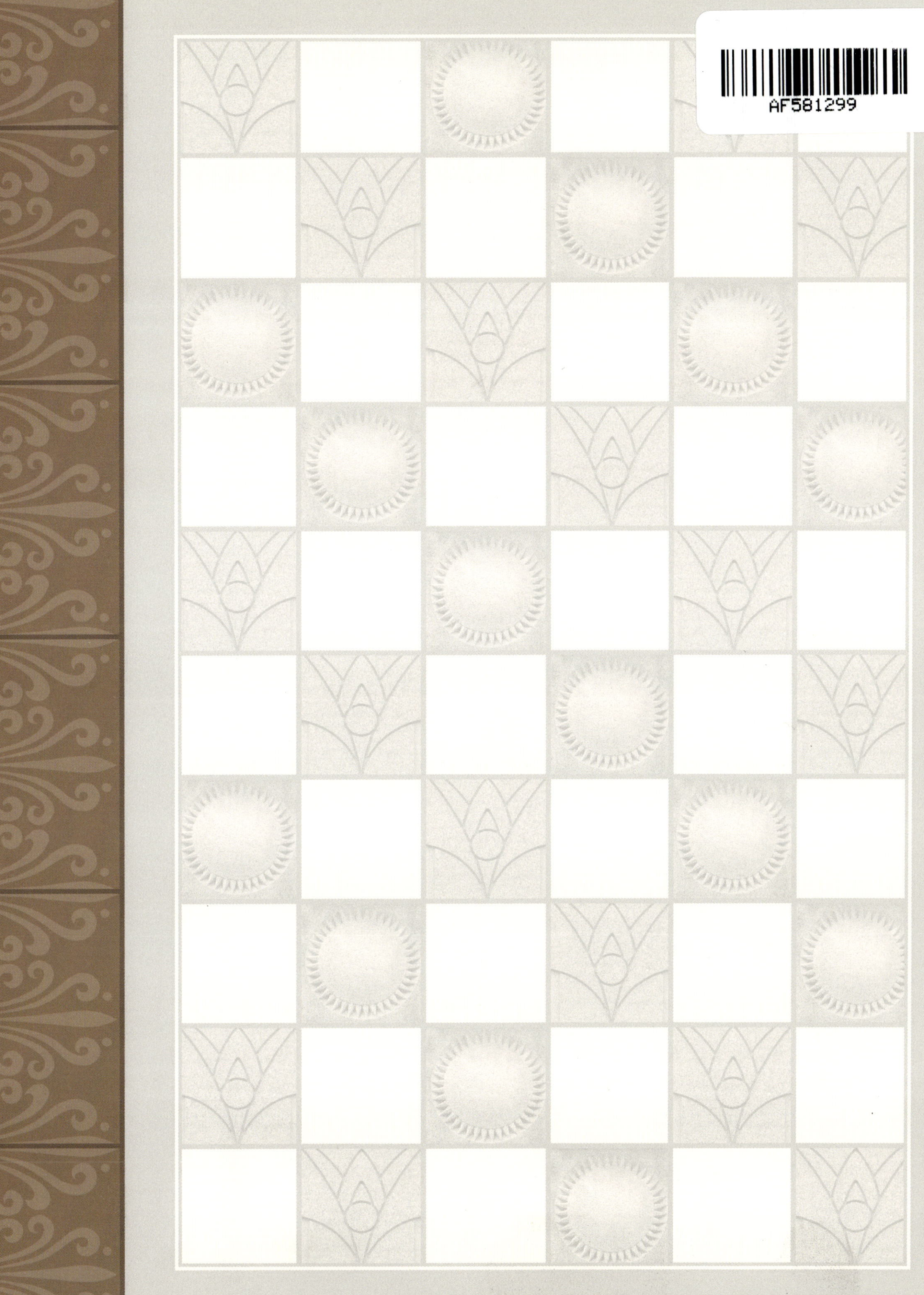

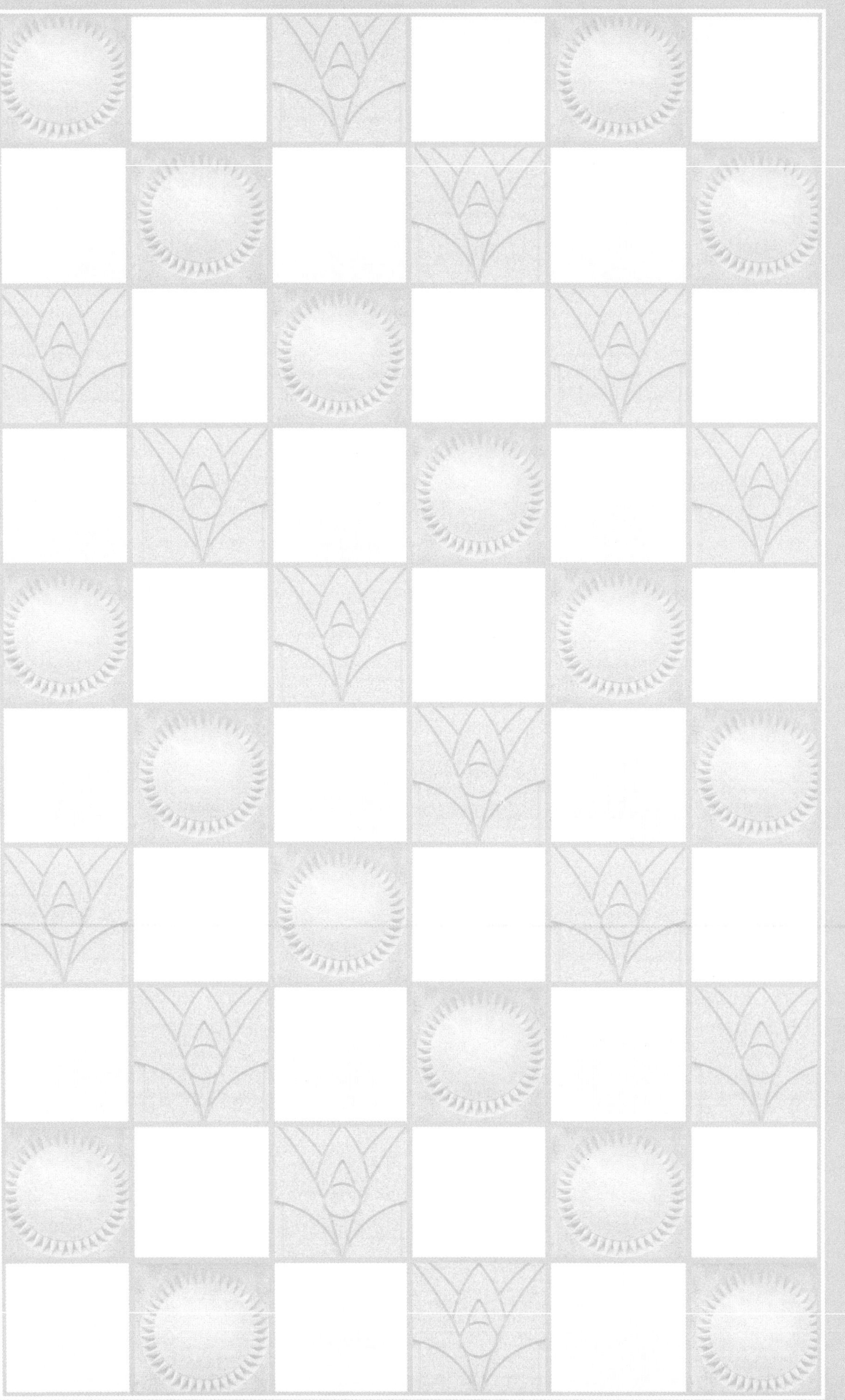

Sacred Walls

Learning from Temple Symbols

To my wife Sharlene, who loves the temple
and makes all good things in my life possible.

Published by Covenant Communications, Inc. American Fork, Utah

Printed in China
First Printing: August 2009

16 15 14 13 12 11 10 09 10 9 8 7 6 5 4

ISBN-13: 978-1-59811-772-1
ISBN-10: 1-59811-772-6

Sacred Walls

Learning from Temple Symbols

Gerald E. Hansen Jr.
photos by Val Brinkerhoff

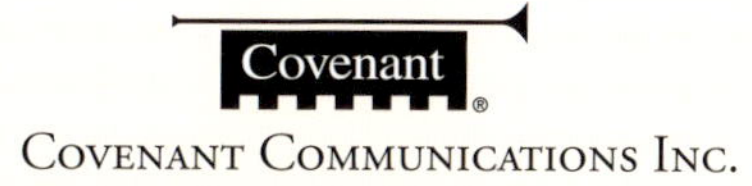

Covenant Communications Inc.

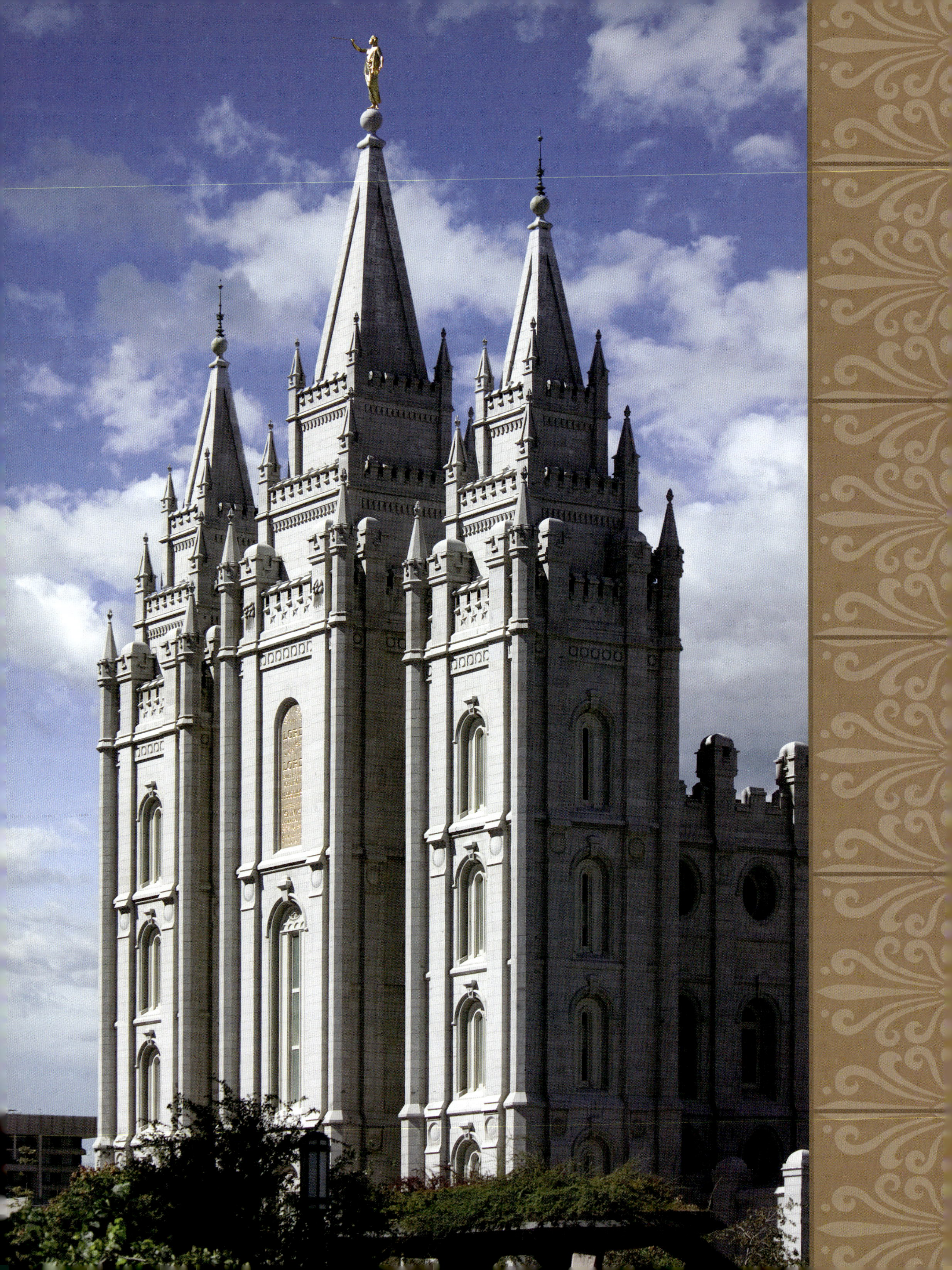

Contents

Preface vii

Introduction ix

Journey to the Tree of Life 1

Palmyra New York Temple 4

The "Good/Evil Contrast" Pattern 9

Manti Utah and Logan Utah Temples 13

Gathering to the Family of God 17

Mesa Arizona Temple 20

Returning to the Tree of Life 25

Boston Massachusetts Temple 31

Covenants and Ascension to God 37

Albuquerque New Mexico Temple 40

Rebirth 43

San Diego California Temple 47

Eternal Perspectives 51

Nauvoo Illinois Temple 54

The Law of the Gospel and the Covenant 59

Mount Timpanogos Utah Temple 63

Entering the Presence of God 67

Oakland California Temple 70

The Gifts of God 75

Salt Lake Temple 78

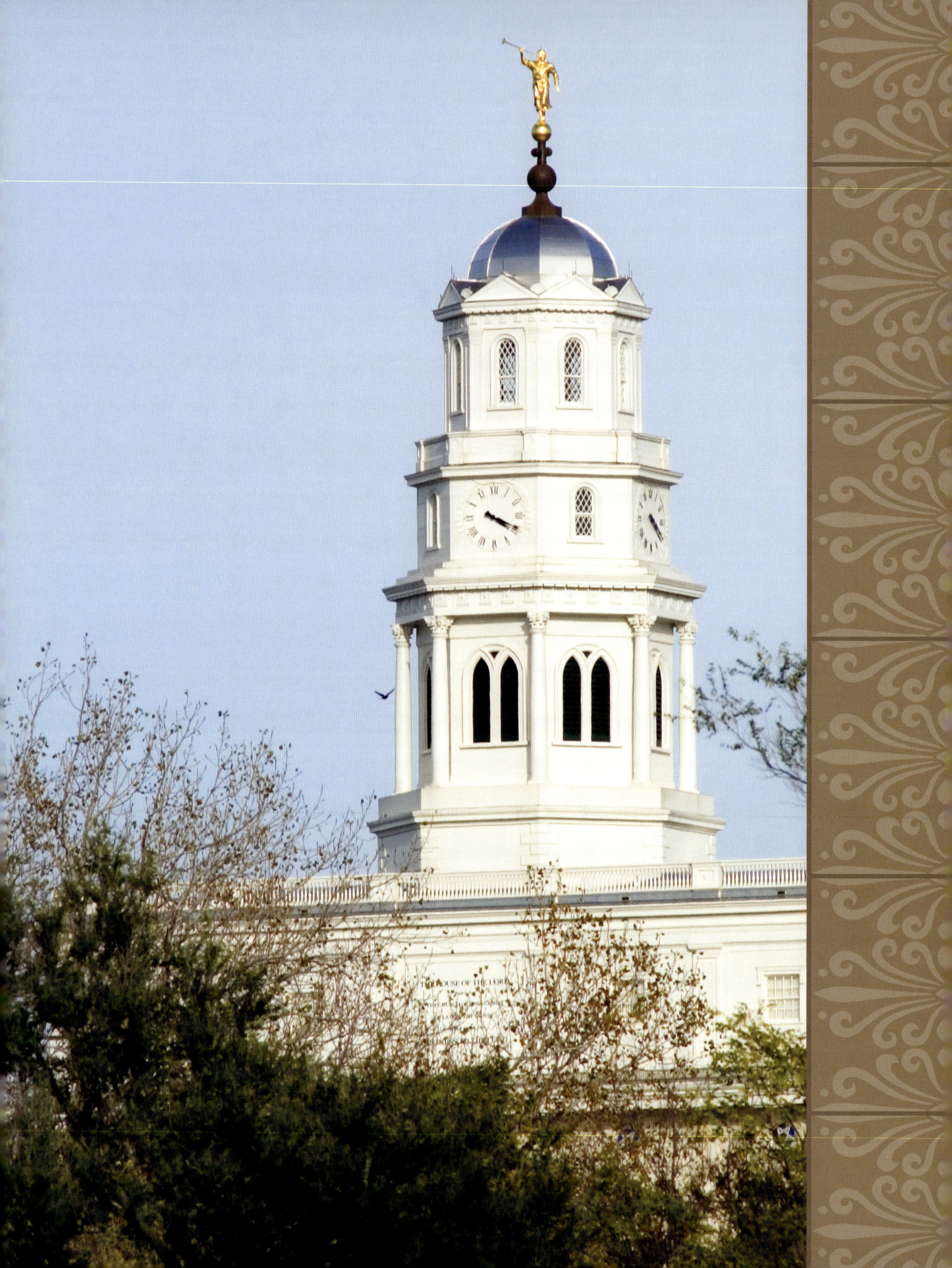

Preface

Latter-day Saints know that they should be careful in how they talk about the details of the temple endowment—not because there is anything shocking or strange about the ceremony, but because it is a personal covenant experience with God and should thus be treated with great respect. It is, therefore, not my intention to say anything that would offend the sensibilities of those who treat their temple blessings with sacred reverence. On the contrary, it is very much my purpose to help temple-going Latter-day Saints be even more grateful for the sacred endowment. In this book I will examine doctrines and principles found in the Book of Mormon that are relevant to the temple and then illustrate those doctrines and principles with images of symbols found on the exterior walls of latter-day temples. I hope that this endeavor will help members of the Church appreciate their temple experience even more profoundly.

Regarding the use of exterior temple symbols, I recognize that all symbols, both written and visual, are open to individual analysis, and I do not claim that my interpretations have exhausted all possibilities. In fact, it is quite the opposite. I have intentionally not examined all aspects of every symbol included nor shown every symbol on the temples considered. I have instead kept this book relatively simple as a sort of primer on temple symbols and doctrines—an introduction for those who have not much noticed these things in the past. It is my hope that this introduction will, accordingly, increase understanding, strengthen testimony, and encourage a desire to visit the temple more often.

—The Author

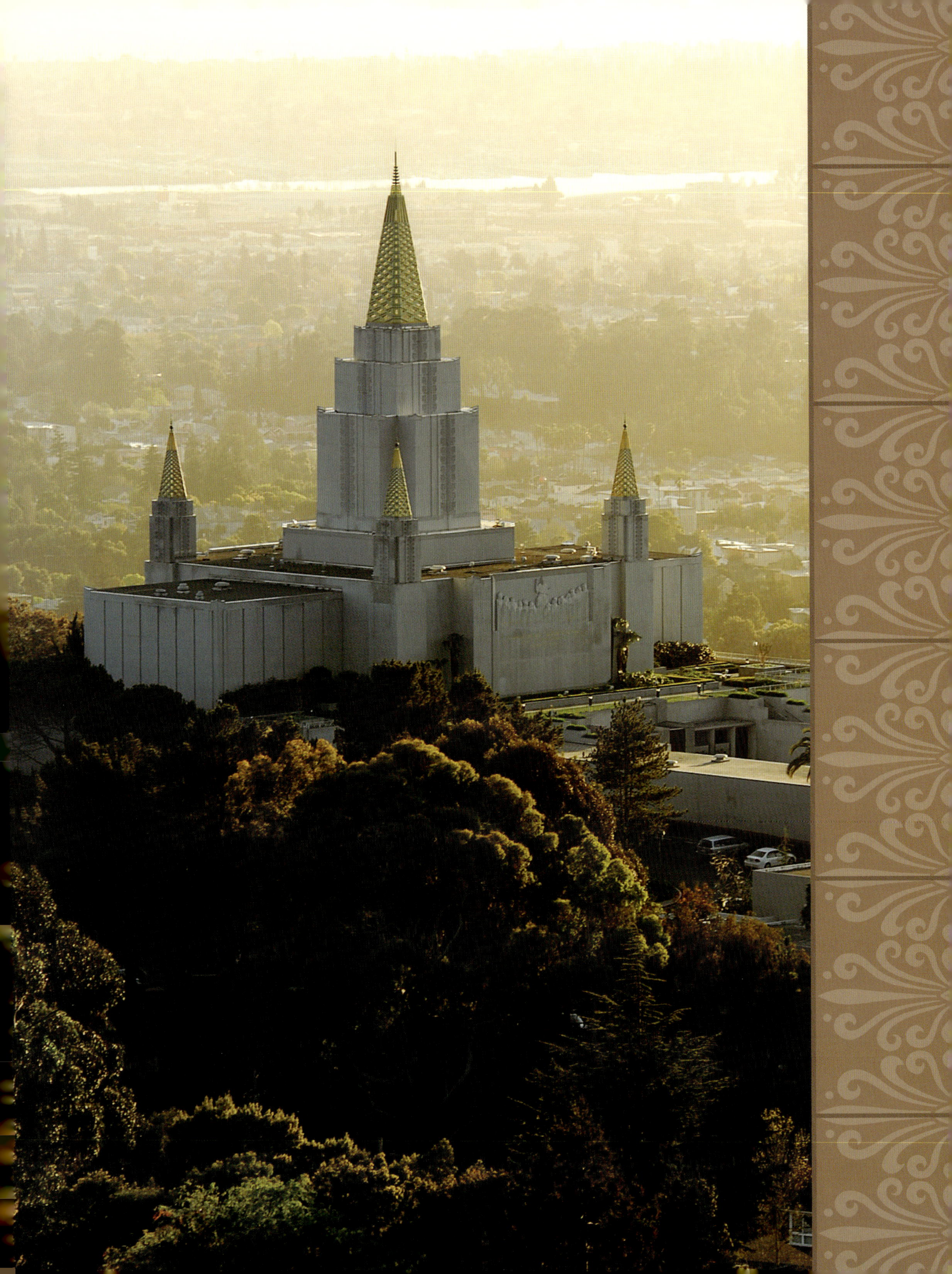

INTRODUCTION

When the angel guided Nephi through his vision of the tree of life (see 1 Nephi 11–14), he showed Nephi, on several occasions, two different images or scenes and then asked him to draw conclusions by comparing the two. In literary terms this technique is called juxtaposition. A great example of juxtaposition from the vision itself occurs when the angel shows Nephi first the tree and then Mary holding the infant Son of God. Seeing these two images one after the other leads Nephi to ask himself the right questions and make the connection in his mind. He comes to understand that the tree symbolizes the love of God.

This book takes an approach similar to the one the angel used with Nephi by juxtaposing Book of Mormon principles and architectural symbols. Each chapter contains an examination in essay form of a sermon or vision in the Book of Mormon that explores gospel principles related to the temple. This essay is immediately followed by a short photo essay of temple exteriors that examines one or two of the main symbolic motifs of a specific temple (or two temples, in the case of chapter two). We believe that the combination of written text and photo essay will generate in the hearts and minds of our readers a greater understanding of and love for the symbolic patterns and doctrines of the temple.

Both books and buildings have voices. Books speak through the written word—by combining alphabetic symbols into words that can be used to denote ideas. Those who love to read inherently understand that through the decipherment of these symbols they can "hear" the words, ideas, and wisdom of both the dead who have long passed on and the living whom they have not yet met. The Nephite prophets, for instance, who wrote the ancient record speak to us today through their writings, as the Book of Mormon itself says they would: "their speech shall whisper out of the dust" (2 Nephi 26:16). In this book we will examine the "voices" of the prophets of the Book of Mormon in order to better understand some of the doctrines of the temple.

Buildings likewise communicate ideas to those who are "listening," though they speak through a different set of symbols. Rather than the letters of an alphabet, buildings use statues and friezes, mosaics and paintings, columns and buttresses, glass and geometric figures, towers and spires, and much more to tell their message. The message of a building may be a little harder to recognize for people in today's world because most of us do not know how to read this symbolic language—it is not widely taught. Still, all buildings have something to say—whether it be about the reason for their existence or the time period in which they were built or the character and beliefs of the people who commissioned them. A building can tell you, for instance, that it is the seat of the government's power or the center of a government's justice system. Another building might suggest that it is a monument to a peoples' imaginative genius. A building may say that its inhabitants want to show off their wealth or that they can barely afford to live. Or it might say that there are wonderful things for you to buy inside, or inexpensive things, or faddish and fashionable things. Buildings can even be used to seduce people to wicked activities or wholesome entertainment. Buildings, like words, can be used to promote causes, to inspire, to provide simple refuge, and to perform specific functions.

Latter-day Saint temples communicate the unique message of the Restoration doctrines. The bulk of this instruction, of course, occurs inside the temples. But the exteriors speak these doctrines as well. In this book we will examine the "voices" of temple exteriors along with the "voices" of the Book of Mormon with the hope that the juxtaposition of the two will increase the joy and understanding of those who love the temples of God. To avoid attempting to rank the symbols or doctrines, we will examine them in the order in which the doctrines appear in the Book of Mormon, beginning with Lehi's vision of the tree of life.

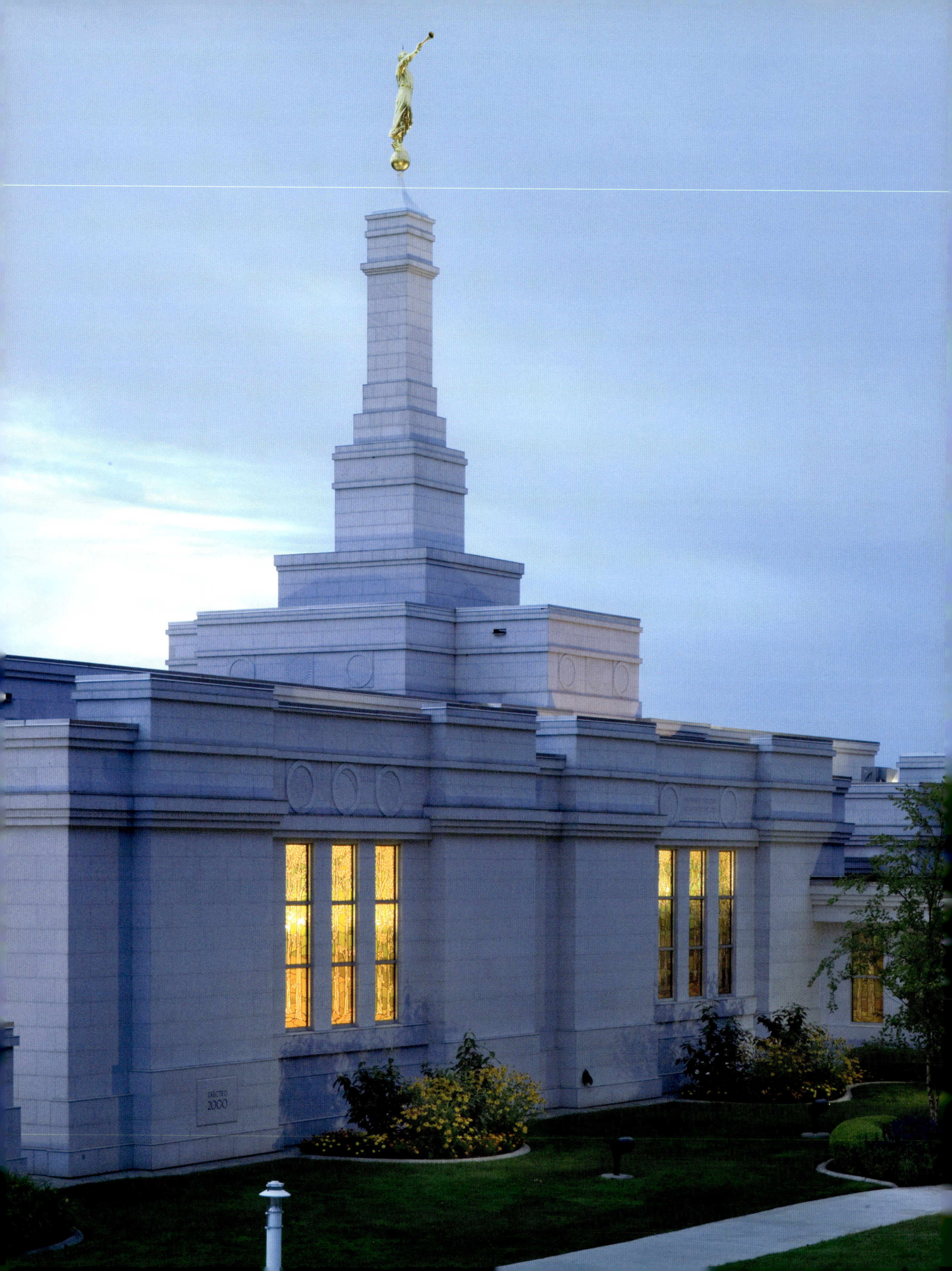
2000

Journey to the Tree of Life

1 Nephi 8

The simplest and most basic pattern of the temple endowment is the long, ascending journey of life that culminates in a final judgment and entrance into God's presence. One of the best explanations of this pattern is this description of the endowment by Elder John A. Widtsoe:

> The endowment given to members of the Church in the temples falls into several divisions. First, there is a course of instruction relative to man's eternal journey from the dim beginning towards his possible glorious destiny. Then, conditions are set up by which that endless journey may be upward in direction. Those who receive this information covenant to obey the laws of eternal progress, and thereby give life to the knowledge received. Finally, it is made clear that a man must sometimes give an account of his deeds, and prove the possession of divine knowledge and religious works. It is a very beautiful, logical and inspiring series of ceremonies.[1]

Put simply, the three main elements of the endowment are, according to Elder Widtsoe, first, instruction on man's eternal journey; second, divine guidance for the journey and the making of covenants to accept this guidance; and third, a final reckoning of behavior on the journey.

The *Encyclopedia of Mormonism* offers an insightful expansion on these basic elements, providing more detail about the nature of the instruction and the divine guidance and implying that the final reckoning will take place in God's presence. In addition, it divides the endowment into four parts rather than three because it includes a preliminary ceremony that Elder Widtsoe does not mention:

> First is the preparatory ordinance, a ceremonial washing and anointing, after which the temple patron dons the sacred clothing of the temple.
>
> Second is a course of instruction by lectures and representations. These include a recital of the most prominent events of the Creation, a figurative depiction of the advent of Adam and Eve and of every man and every woman, the entry of Adam and Eve into the Garden of Eden, the consequent expulsion from the garden, their condition in the world, and their receiving of the Plan of Salvation leading to the return to the presence of God (Talmage, pp. 83–84). . . .
>
> Third is making covenants. . . . Temple covenants give "tests by which one's willingness and fitness for righteousness may be known" (Widtsoe, p. 335). They include the "covenant and promise to observe the law of strict virtue and chastity, to be charitable, benevolent,

> tolerant and pure; to devote both talent and material means to the spread of truth and the uplifting of the [human] race; to maintain devotion to the cause of truth; and to seek in every way to contribute to the great preparation that the earth may be made ready to receive Jesus Christ" (Talmage, p. 84). . . .
>
> Fourth is a sense of divine presence. . . . Temple ordinances are seen as a means for receiving inspiration and instruction through the Holy Spirit, and for preparing to return to the presence of God.[2]

Among the important insights of the *Encyclopedia*'s expansion are, first, the idea that the instruction explaining man's eternal journey is done by means of stories and figurative representations; second, that the divine guidance needed to make the journey a success is often connected to the giving of covenants; and finally, that if a person succeeds on the journey the reward is permission to enter into God's presence. Both simple and complex at the same time, the endowment is a religious ritual that inspires, teaches, and qualifies.

In subtle ways, the scriptures occasionally give instruction on the endowment. The three main elements of the endowment—instruction concerning the eternal journey, divine guidance and covenant making, and entrance into the presence of God—do appear in sacred writ, though usually not in the same form as depicted in the modern temple endowment. In the Book of Mormon, there is no better place to search for temple patterns than in Lehi's dream/vision of the tree of life. In fact, in his revelation, the "journey explanation–divine guidance–entrance into God's presence" pattern occurs twice—once for Lehi and once, later in the same vision, for his family.

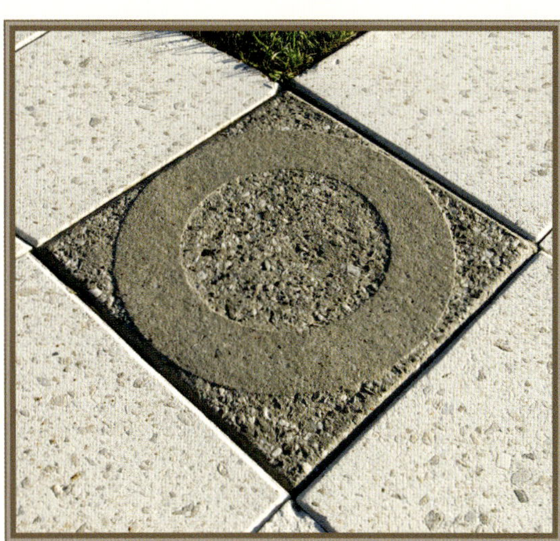

At the beginning of the vision, Lehi journeys through a "dark and dreary wilderness" (1 Nephi 8:4), which is a representation of the lone and dreary world and also a symbol of the test of mortality. At this point the record does not include the normal instruction concerning man's eternal journey. That will come later in the vision with the description of the types of temptation that lead people away from the tree. For the moment, all the record shows is that Lehi is on the journey. The second part of the endowment pattern, the divine guidance, is also abbreviated until later, but it is worth noting that a divine guide dressed in white appears and leads Lehi through the dark and dreary waste (see 1 Nephi 8:5–7). In the third part of the endowment process, entrance into God's presence, Lehi moves through three degrees of sacredness—from a less sacred space to a sacred space and finally to a most sacred space.

This threefold journey follows the basic pattern of progression toward the sacred that occurs in all temples. In ancient times, the outer court of the tabernacle of Moses was considered less sacred space. Temples today likewise have less sacred areas—the grounds, waiting rooms, dressing rooms, baptismal fonts, and chapels. Then there is an inner court that is more sacred and, therefore, more restricted—the Holy Place in the tabernacle of Moses and the endowment rooms in modern temples. Finally, there is a most sacred area that patrons must learn how to reach through the endowment. In the tabernacle of Moses, this was the Holy of Holies. In a modern temple it is the celestial room.

Lehi's endowment experience follows this same pattern. After traveling for many hours through the dark and dreary waste—obviously a less sacred space—he prays to God for mercy and is delivered into a more sacred space, represented by a large and spacious field where the tree of life is located. The tree itself represents the most sacred space. In fact, it represents Jesus Christ and His Atonement. By partaking of the tree's fruit, Lehi symbolically stands in God's presence and partakes of His love (see 1 Nephi 8:8–11).

It should not be missed that prayer is the key for Lehi's move from a less sacred space to a sacred space to the most sacred space. The symbolism used in the tabernacle of Moses likewise emphasized the importance of prayer. In the tabernacle, all of the furniture symbolized parts of the plan of salvation and the types of righteousness that a person had to attain to prepare for God's presence. The wash basin in the outer court, for instance, represented being washed clean of sin, and the candelabrum in the Holy Place represented living by the inspiration of the Holy Ghost. As the high priest of Israel moved from the outer court to the inner court, then through the veil, and finally into the most Holy of Holies, he vicariously represented for the people the journey that they must make through the plan of salvation to prepare to enter God's presence. It is noteworthy that the final piece of furniture, situated directly in front of the veil separating the Holy Place from the Holy of Holies, was the altar of incense, representing the power of prayer. Thus the entrance through the veil was symbolically achieved through prayer—through a request—as it was with the brother of Jared (see Ether 3:10), to come into God's presence. Lehi's prayer was likewise the key to his entrance into God's presence.

In the second recital of the temple pattern in Lehi's vision, the journey of Sariah, Nephi, and Sam is stalled at the head of the river running farther on near the tree. Sariah and her two sons do not know where to go. Lehi himself acts as their divine guide, beckoning to them and calling to them until they also come and symbolically enter into God's presence by partaking of the fruit of the tree (see 1 Nephi 8:13–16). Lehi then calls to Laman and Lemuel and beckons to

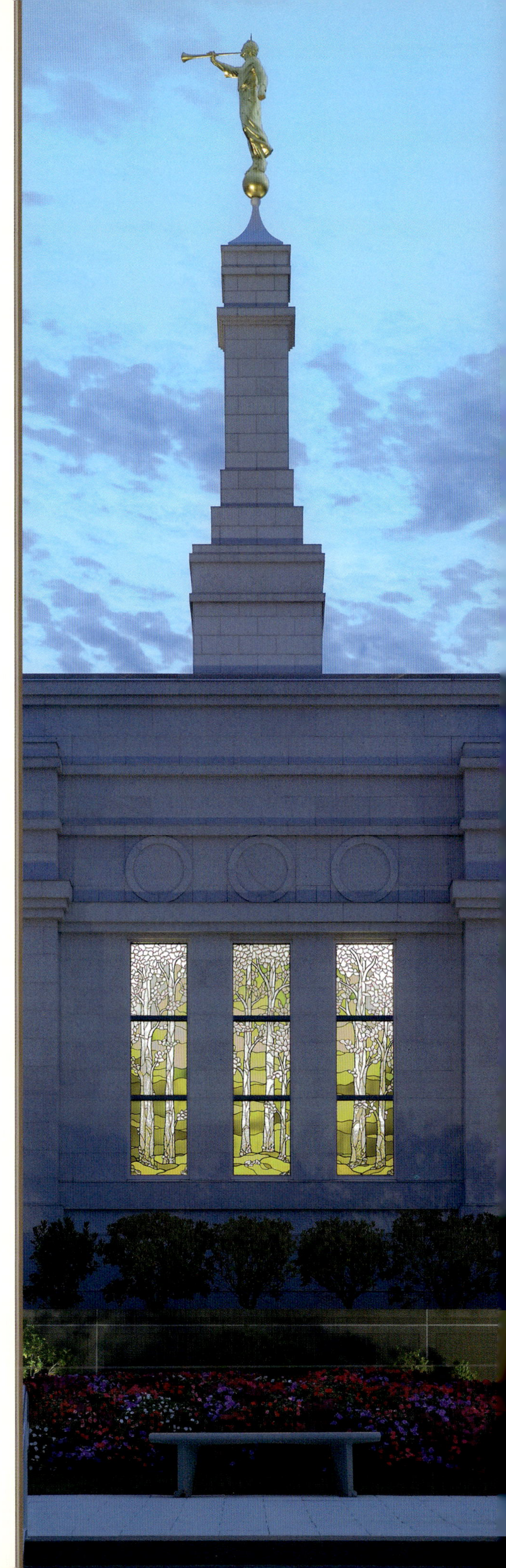

Palmyra New York Temple

Journey to the Tree of Life

Latter-day Saints at the Palmyra New York Temple begin the symbolic journey to God on a distinctive cement path leading to the east entrance. As they climb upward from the parking lot, they see several dozen squared circles at intervals on the outer edges of the path. The joining of a circle with a square is a worldwide symbol that for centuries has symbolized the meeting of heaven and earth at holy places, the circle representing the dome of heaven and the square representing the four corners of the earth. This repeated symbol encourages temple-goers to keep moving as it reminds them of their purpose, which is to meet with God in His holy house. Granted, this encounter with God in the temple happens not literally but symbolically and through the Holy Ghost, but all temple patrons should know and believe that their temple experience is preparation for a future day when they will literally meet Heavenly Father and experience His love.

Temples teach God's children how to become like Him—how to become sanctified and holy beings. The squared circle appropriately symbolizes that human beings are made from the dust of this earth and are mortal but that they also have the potential to become divine if they will only join with God through at-one-ment and by covenant.

Continuing along the path, temple patrons arrive at a large octagon just in front of the east entrance. (There is also one on the west overlooking the Sacred Grove.) Like the squared circle, this symbol is also centuries old. In Christian tradition, the eight sides of the octagon, found particularly in baptistries, signify spiritual rebirth and resurrection. The common explanation for this meaning is that the eight sides represent the spiritual creation that occurred on the imaginary eighth day, the day after the seven days of the physical creation of the earth. As a temple symbol, the octagon thus fittingly represents the need of all patrons to change from fallen mortals to sanctified, celestial beings.

A few steps past the octagon bring temple-goers to the entrance doors, made of stained-glass and decorated with a grouping of trees, which represents the trees of the garden. The second tree from the left bears five circular, multifaceted fruits that stand out from the flat-textured leaves surrounding them. Since the number five often represents man,[3] this tree undoubtedly symbolizes the tree of knowledge of good and evil—the tree that made Adam and Eve mortal. Thus, all who enter the temple through these beautiful glass doors are powerfully reminded that they have partaken of the effects of the Fall of Adam and Eve. They are mortal and natural, and they need a Savior to grant them immortality and make eternal life possible. For those who realize such dependency, the temple is the absolute best place to go for help because the Atonement is the central and all-pervasive theme of the temple endowment. The endowment instructs God's children that they must change from their natural, fallen character and take upon themselves the nature of God through the power of Christ's Atonement. It also shows them how Satan works to prevent them from pursuing true repentance. Finally, it gives them faith and hope that they can make the ascension to God and godliness because of the grace and mercy of Heavenly Father and His Son.

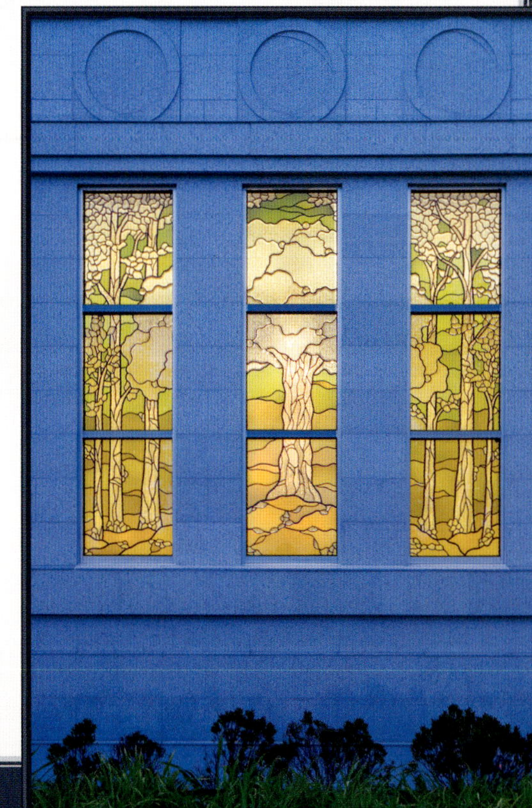

In the Palmyra Temple, this grace and mercy are most beautifully represented by a brilliant depiction of the tree of life in the large stained-glass window in the celestial room, which symbolically completes the journey back to God. Twelve bright, multifaceted crystal fruits hang on the tree. Historically, the number twelve symbolizes the union of the temporal with the spiritual (the joining of heaven and earth) and the fruits of the tree of life.[4] In the case of the Palmyra Temple window, the number twelve would certainly also signify that the priesthood of God administers the ordinances of exaltation. It also calls to mind the gathering of the tribes of Israel, a reminder that true Israel consists of all those who have received and honored temple covenants.

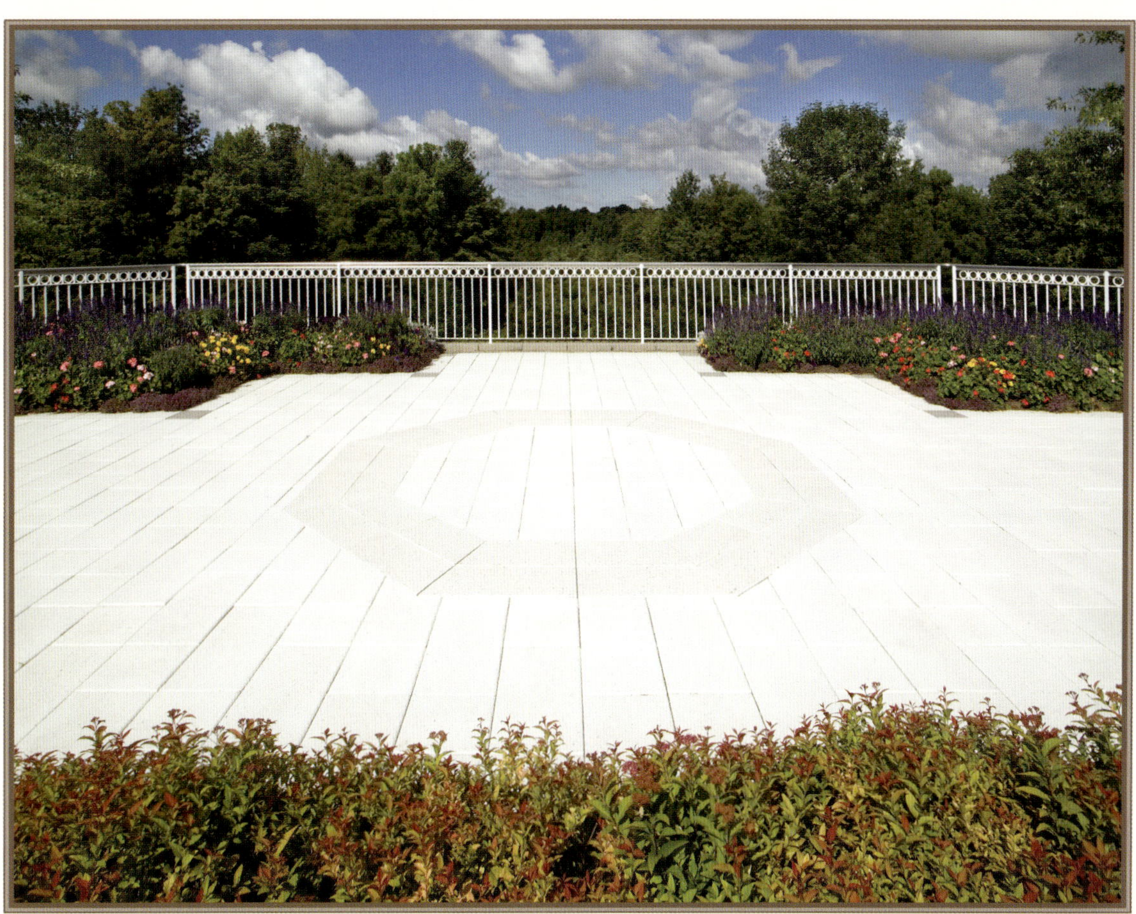

them to come as well, but they refuse to accept his guidance (see 1 Nephi 8:17–18).

It is at this point that the vision expands to give instruction on the eternal journey. It describes certain types of dangers inherent to mortality and recommends the word of God, symbolized by the rod of iron, as the means of deliverance from those dangers. This is important information for anyone battling evil and, therefore, an important part of the instruction of any endowment.

Lehi learns that although vast numbers of people begin their journey with every intention of seeking the tree (see 1 Nephi 8:20–21), many neglect the divine help offered in the form of the iron rod and consequently end up wandering into forbidden paths. Blinded in the confusion of the mists of darkness, they lose their way and are lost (see 1 Nephi 8:23). Although a second group of individuals does accept the proffered help and find God, a significant number of them are lost as they also eventually reject the divine guidance because of persecution and pressure from other people (see 1 Nephi 8:24–28).

A third large group of people journey through life with very little desire to know God. From the beginning, these people intentionally seek the great and spacious building (see 1 Nephi 8:31), with apparently no desire to partake of the fruit of the tree. Rather than being motivated by the love of God, they are drawn to the "pride of the world" (1 Nephi 11:36), possibly the very best of Satan's many temptations. Some of this group wander off and are lost, showing that the promise of wealth and power often disappoints (see 1 Nephi 8:32). Even worse, many of this third group obtain their goal, enter the building, and then become agents of evil themselves by persecuting those who are at the tree (see 1 Nephi 8:27, 33).

A great river separates the tree and the building (see 1 Nephi 8:13–14), signifying that one cannot get to the tree from the building except by repentance—by leaving the building, returning to the head of the river, grabbing onto the rod, and following the path to the tree. Only by this change of heart and reversal of direction can these people partake of the fruit. Without repentance, without forsaking "the things of this world" and the "honors of men" (D&C 121:35), there is no way to get to the tree.

Finally, Lehi learns of a fourth group of individuals who reach the tree, do not let go of the rod of iron, and persist in the path of righteousness. This group represents those who come into the presence of God and receive eternal life. They humbly accept God's help and do not take it for granted (see 1 Nephi 8:30).

Like all symbols, the rod of iron can have several levels of meaning. The most common interpretation of the rod, however, is that it is symbolic of the word of God, which is found in the scriptures and the teachings of modern prophets. The following statement by Elder Rudger Clawson excellently summarizes this application:

> We are a greatly blessed people, but we find ourselves in a world that is sometimes designated as "the lone and dreary world," and as we pass along we encounter many dangerous pitfalls, but the Lord in heaven has provided a guide to take us safely through.
>
> Let me draw your attention to the fact that we have four great and important books, comprising the standard works of the Church namely, the Bible, the Book of Mormon, the D&C, and the Pearl of Great Price. These four precious volumes which contain the word of God to the children of men constitute the best library in all the world. . . .
>
> In connection with these important books that mean so much and are of such inestimable value to the Latter-day Saints, we have the gift of the Holy Ghost. . . .
>
> In addition to all this, as constituting a sure guide, we have the living oracles of the Church. The prophets in the meridian of time have spoken to us, and now the prophets of the latter days speak.[5]

Elder Clawson clearly wants members of the Church to know that they have the divine guidance necessary to navigate the temptations of Satan and "the lone and dreary world." Lehi's vision makes it plain that desire, determination, acceptance of divine help, and persistence lead to the joy of partaking of the fruit of the tree of life.

In summary, the endowment of knowledge that Lehi receives in his dream/vision follows the basic pattern that Elder Widstoe and the *Encyclopedia of Mormonism* suggest make up the modern endowment: first, Lehi learns through symbolism how Satan seduces and tempts God's children; next, he receives divine guidance from a messenger from Heavenly Father for his journey through life; and finally, he enters the presence of God, symbolized by partaking of the fruit of the tree. Lehi's dream admittedly uses a different structure and different figurative images from those used in the modern endowment, but the explanation of the eternal journey, the divine guidance for that journey, and the assurance of eventual entrance into God's presence all play major parts in the vision.

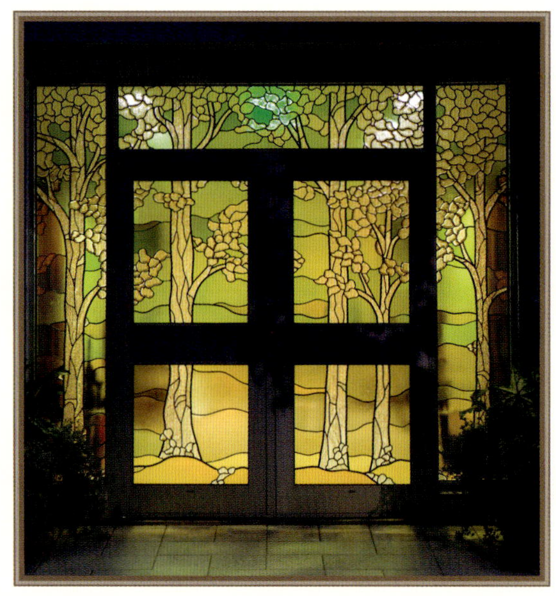

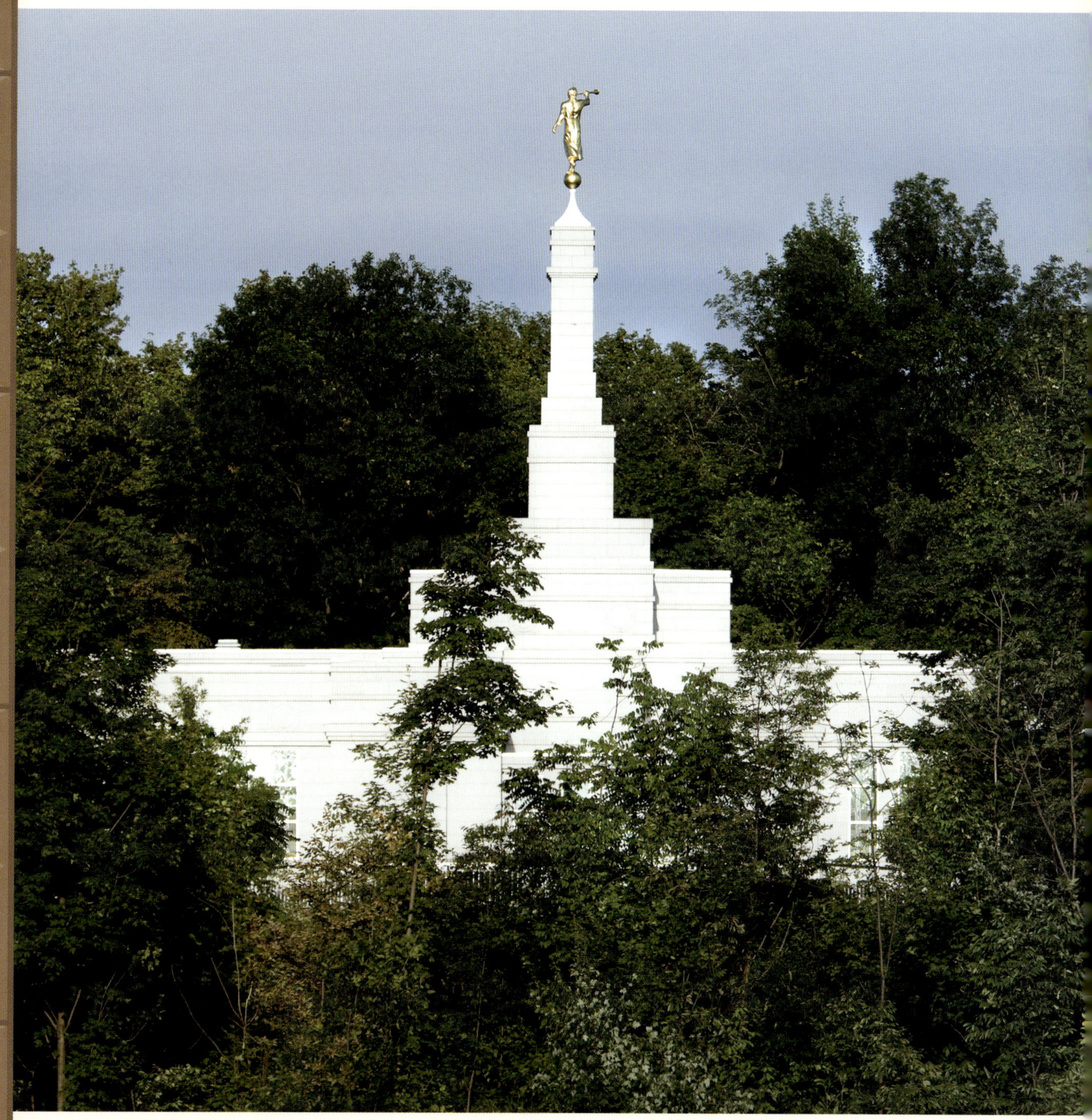

The significance of Lehi's vision being at the beginning of the Book of Mormon can hardly be overestimated. It sets the stage for all that follows. A great many of the events, episodes, and stories that follow it portray the struggles and consequences of the fundamental mortal choice between good and evil, represented respectively by the tree of life and the great and spacious building. In this regard, the vision functions like the temple endowment because everything that follows it—life, in the case of the temple, and the rest of the Book of Mormon, in the case of Lehi's dream—should be analyzed through the moral template that it establishes and dramatizes.

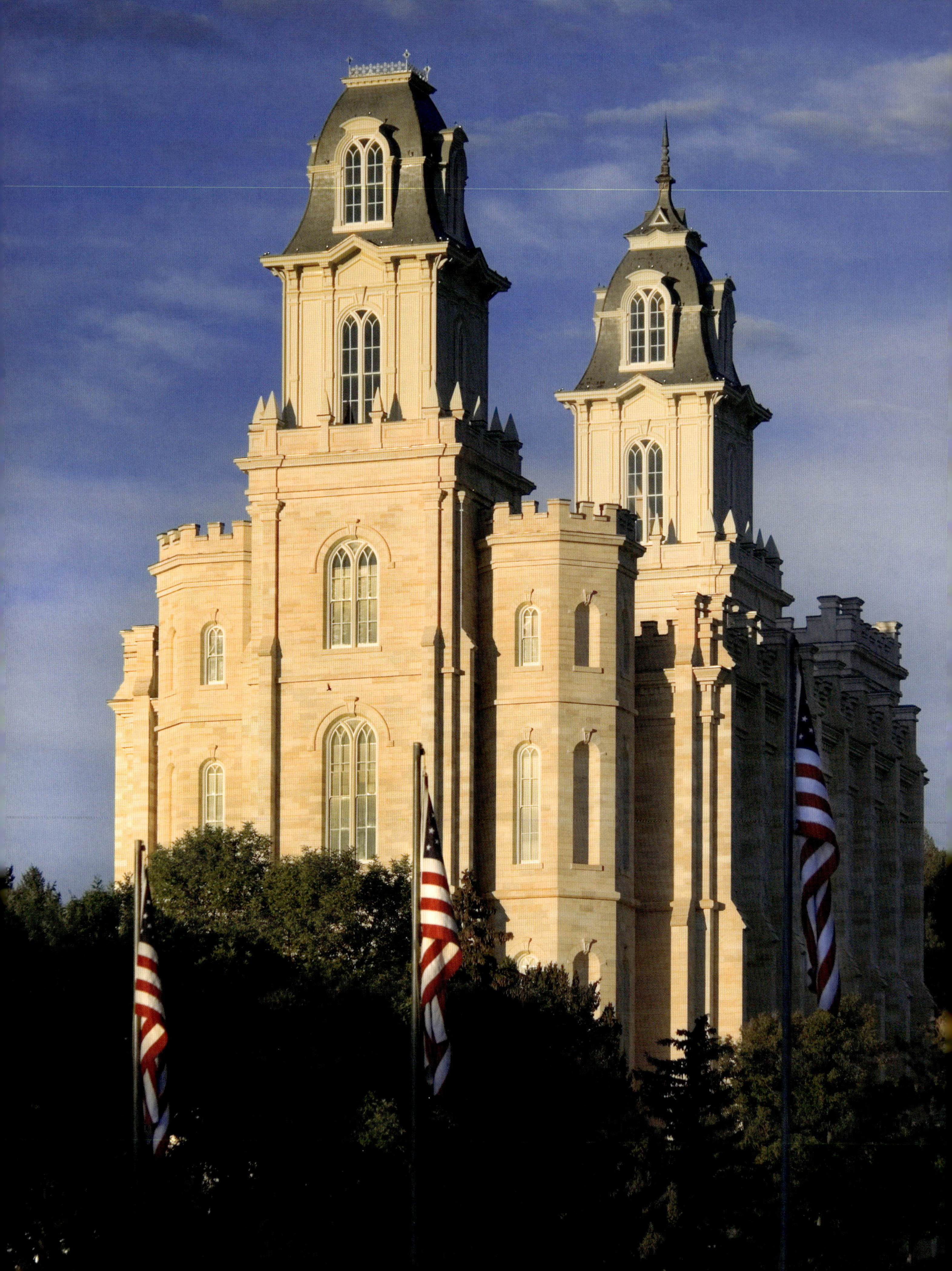

The "Good/Evil Contrast" Pattern

Protection in the War Against Satan

1 Nephi 11—14

Temples teach the Saints profound truths about God; they also teach about the devious nature of Satan's temptations. In the endowment ceremony, the purpose for this instruction is to help God's children judge wisely between the greater power of God and the seductions of Satan. A wonderful scriptural example of this teaching method is Moses' vision first of God and then of the devil. When God addresses Moses, He calls him "my son," stressing Moses' potential to eventually become like his Heavenly Father. Satan, on the other hand, calls Moses "son of man" in an effort to demean him and make him doubt his true nature and destiny. In Moses' case, the devil's temptation does not work: the contrast of God's glory and power is more than sufficient for Moses to judge between God and Satan and decide to dismiss the latter (see Moses 1:1–22).

Moses' experience is not unique. On the contrary, this "see God/see Satan" pattern, or possibly better named the "good/evil contrast" pattern, occurs often in scripture and in life. Among the most profound and powerful examples of this pattern in the Book of Mormon is Nephi's vision of the tree of life. This vision offers a remarkable endowment of knowledge concerning Satan's tactics and what God has done to help us see through them and overcome them.

There are four main parts to Nephi's vision: two act as bookends to introduce and reiterate the main point, and two provide the meat of the instruction. Part one uses symbols to show that the basic choice in life is between serving God and serving Satan; part two recounts the history of the Nephites as an example of the consequences for choosing to serve Satan; part three prescribes an antidote to Satan's temptations; and part four uses a new set of symbols to reemphasize that serving God or serving Satan is the basic choice of life.

Part one opens with the Spirit of the Lord and an angel acting as divine guides for Nephi, showing him the main symbols of his father's vision. Nephi sees the tree of life, the rod of iron, and the great and spacious building. With help from the angel, he discerns the meaning of each of these symbols. The tree represents the love of God, the rod of iron represents the word of God, and the great and spacious building represents the pride of the world. Through the first two symbols, Nephi learns that God's methods for fighting the battle against evil are love and sacrifice. He learns that God's love is so deep that He condescends to send His

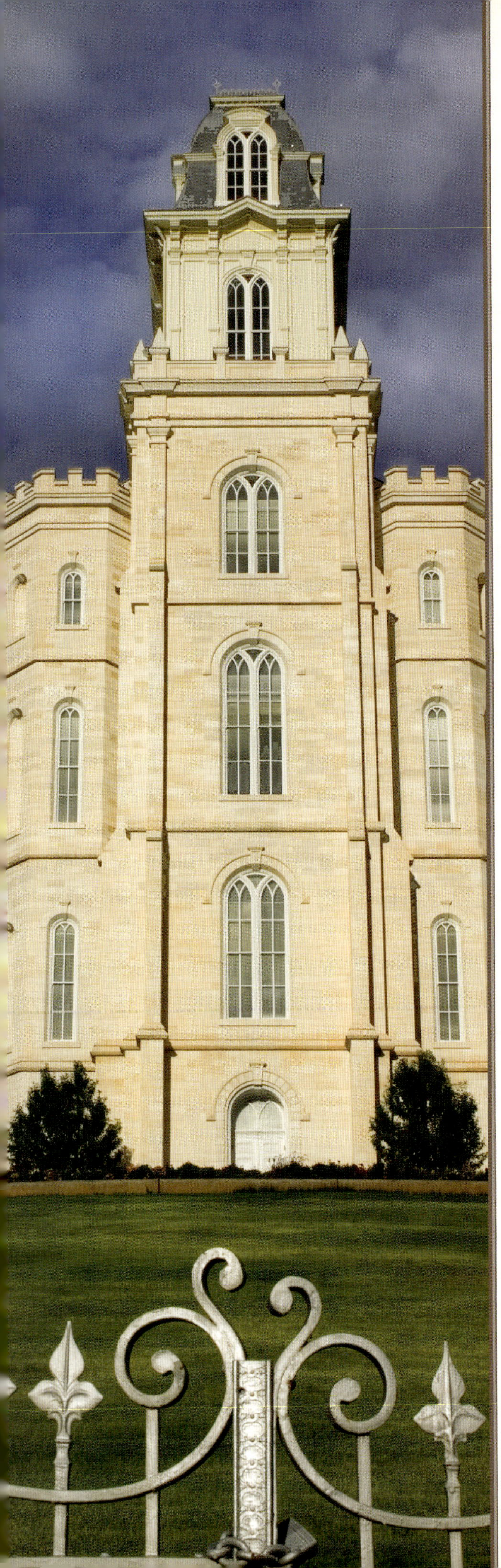

Only Begotten Son to earth to atone for the sins of His imperfect children. Nephi learns that through God's Son, God teaches His children, ministers to their needs, and invites them to come back to His presence. In contrast, by the symbol of the great and spacious building, Nephi sees that Satan's methods are violence and selfishness. He learns that, because of pride, Satan and his followers fight against God, His Son, and His Apostles. At the end of this portion of the vision, Nephi happily learns that Satan will eventually lose the battle and wickedness will be destroyed (see 1 Nephi 11:36).

Part two of the vision uses a thumbnail sketch of the thousand years of Nephite history as an example of a nation that chose evil—a nation that symbolically chose the building instead of the tree—and as a result was destroyed. Though God blessed the Nephites, even to the point that He allowed them to see Christ and appointed twelve disciples to minister to them, they still filled their history with wars and contentions until they were entirely wiped out. The causes of this destruction were the temptations of the devil and the vain imaginations and pride of the children of men, respectively symbolized in the vision by the mists of darkness and the large and spacious building (see 1 Nephi 12:17–18). These two symbols show that the source of the Nephites' downfall was partly the devil (the mists of darkness), but it was also partly their own natural-man desires (the building). The Nephites were blinded by Satan's deceptions, but they also willingly let their own imaginations increase the depth of their blindness. The message of this part of Nephi's vision seems very clear: the destruction of the Nephite nation symbolizes the fate of peoples and individuals who make the wrong choice in life—who choose to follow Satan instead of God. The vision cautions modern readers against blindness and self-deception, warning us to choose the tree, not the building.

Part three of Nephi's vision intensifies the warning and illuminates the particulars of the two choices, and it does so with significant symbolic representations, as in any endowment process. It is here that Nephi learns more particularly concerning the tactics of Satan. This part of the vision is the story of the Gentile nations (see 1 Nephi 13:3)[6] and is especially useful to Latter-day Saints because it is the story of the temptations of modern society—our story and our temptations—whether we live in the United States, Brazil, Germany, Tonga, Japan, or anywhere else. It should be noted that a history of the Gentile nations could contain an endless amount of material from numberless lands and time periods and could be interminably long. But Nephi's vision includes only a highly selective account that concentrates on salvational history. After it outlines the great temptations that exist in any modern society, it primarily focuses on the antidote for the temptations of Satan—the covenants and doctrines of God and the Book of Mormon—and describes the events that led to the Restoration through Joseph Smith. It is the most insightful portion of Nephi's instructive experience and the focal point of the "good/evil contrast" discourse.

The great symbol in this part of the vision for Satan's temptations in modern society is a great and abominable church that yokes the Saints with a yoke of iron. Later in the vision, Nephi describes this "church" as "the mother of abominations" and "the whore of all the earth" (1 Nephi 14:10). These designations are particularly descriptive of the pernicious nature of the worldly desires that he associates with this symbolic church. The desire for riches, power, and the praise of men is indeed the mother, or greatest source, of other sins. Wealth, power, and prestige are so seductive that many otherwise good people sacrifice family relations, church responsibilities, personal integrity, and other sacred possessions to pursue them. We see these desires leading the Nephites away from God again and again. Mormon placed them first in his list of the sins that caused the loss of Nephite lands at the time of Helaman (see Helaman 4:12), and Moroni declared that it was the pursuit of power and money and the consequent rise of secret combinations that destroyed both the Nephite and Jaredite civilizations (see Ether 8:22).

The desire for wealth seems to encompass the other two desires, for with great wealth come power and prestige. Indeed, Satan seeks to convince the children of men that they can buy happiness if they can just acquire enough money. Thus, the desire for wealth is the "mother of abominations,"

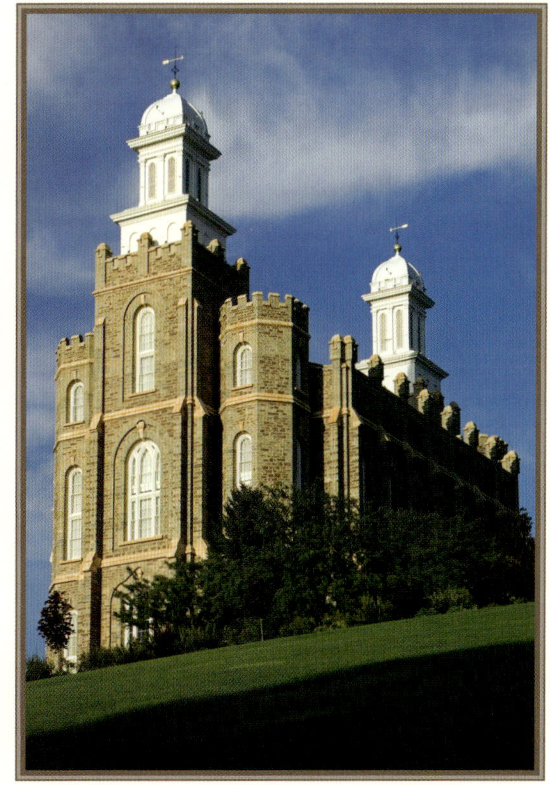

or, as Paul famously declares, "the love of money is the root of all evil" (1 Timothy 6:10).

Having seen and understood the disease, Nephi is now ready to learn about the most crucial part of the "good/evil contrast." The angel shows him the antidote God has prepared: acceptance of and adherence to the principles of the Book of Mormon. Under the angel's tutelage, Nephi learns that an important precursor to the bringing forth of the Book of Mormon was the preparation of a nation where the restoration of the fullness of the gospel could take place. The angel explains this process by presenting Nephi with a short list of some of the events that played a part in the establishment of the United States of America as a modern nation, including the discovery of the new world by Columbus (see 1 Nephi 13:12), early colonization (see 1 Nephi 13:13–15), and the Revolutionary War (see 1 Nephi 13:16–19). This short history does not mean that the United States and its citizens are arbitrarily dearer to God than other nations and peoples, but rather that God molded a new country into a place of religious freedom for the purpose of establishing a viable environment for the restoration of His gospel. The political customs and systems in place in nineteenth-century America provided the ideal environment in which the restored Church could expand and flourish.

After seeing the establishment of a place for the Restoration, Nephi witnesses the coming forth of the Book of Mormon. He learns that the book will play an integral part in the Restoration by restoring crucial parts of the gospel that were lost. The angel explains to him that the record of the Jews originally contained the fullness of the gospel and went forth "in purity unto the Gentiles" (1 Nephi 13:25), but

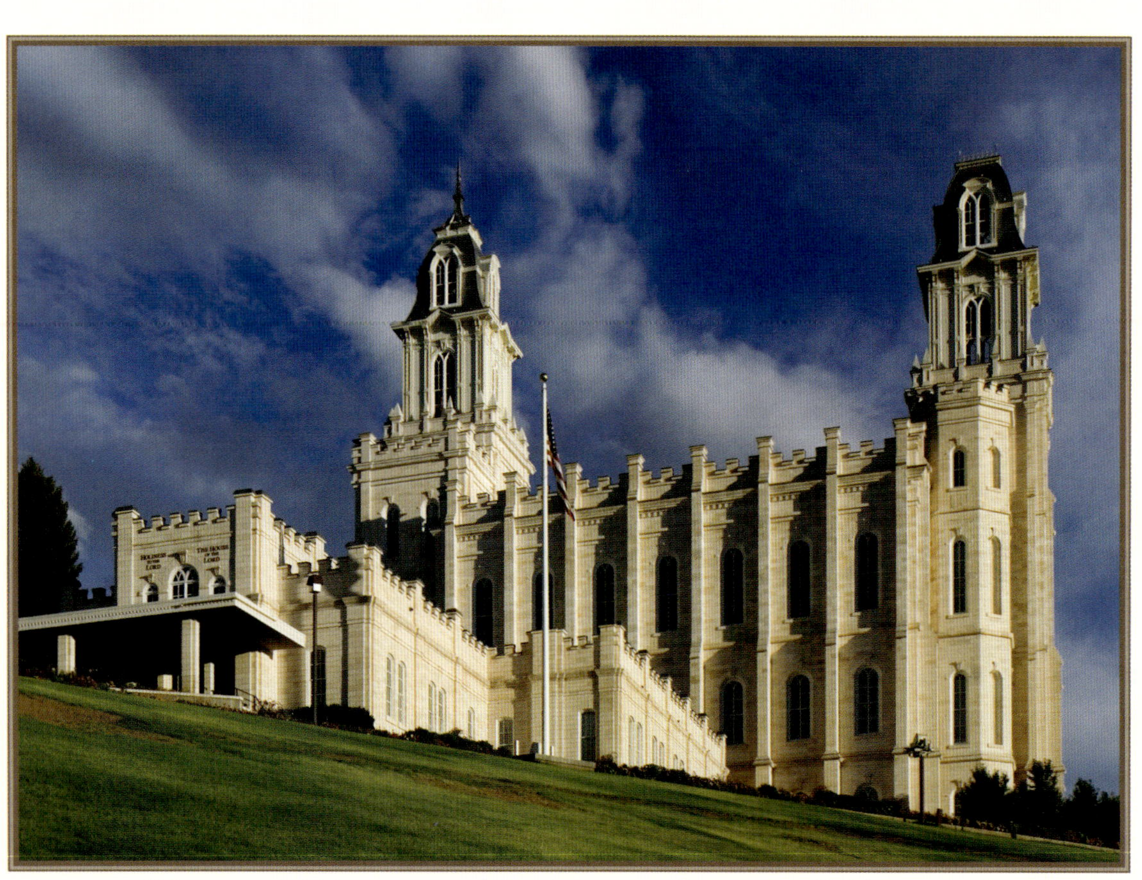

Manti Utah and Logan Utah Temples

Fortresses for Good and Protection from Evil

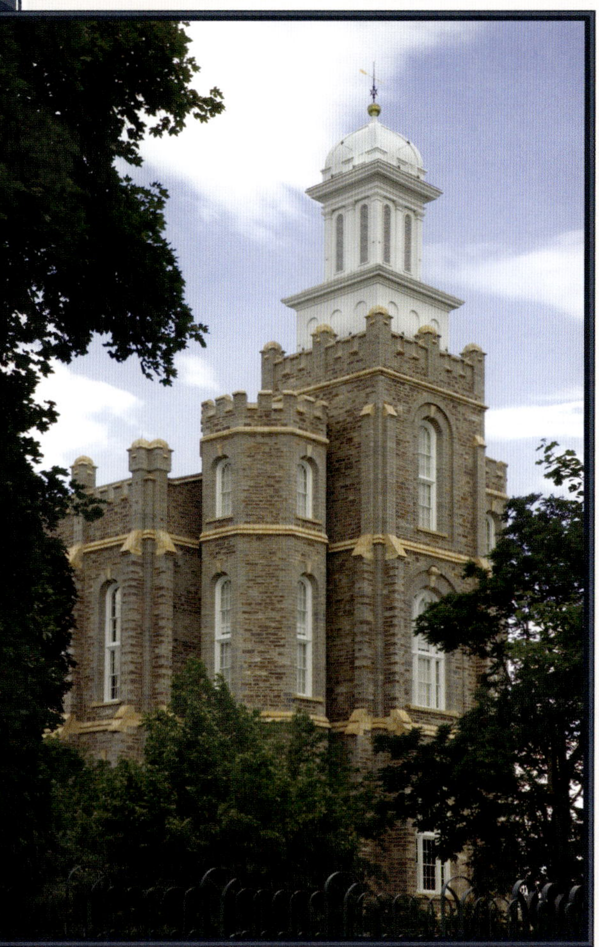

"A mighty fortress is our God," proclaims the hymn by Martin Luther, "A tower of strength ne'er failing. A helper mighty is our God, O'er ills of life prevailing" (*Hymns,* 68). Just as this hymn inspires us to trust in God, so the temples in Logan and Manti, Utah, call us to remember God's promises to protect and help His children.

The turrets (the rounded towers seen on both sides of the central towers) and battlements of these sacred buildings boldly declare that these edifices are the fortresses of God and that all who have entered therein and who honor Him by keeping His covenants will have His protection from evil and His help in their trials. The symbolic design of these formidable structures is fairly simple but effective. The solid walls are made to resemble ancient castles inside which the Saints can gather for safety. Recalling medieval fortifications built on hills, these spiritual fortresses overlook their respective valleys and thus symbolically proclaim that they can warn us of dangers and attacks by the evil one. They are the abode of our Lord, and we owe Him our allegiance. If we are faithful to Him, He will direct us in our spiritual battles and help us vanquish our foes. These majestic pioneer temples testify that God has given us the endowment to arm us against the forces of evil and to help protect us in our spiritual battles.

The endowment safeguards the Saints in at least two magnificent ways. First, there is an actual gift of promised spiritual protection for those who will honor God and His covenants. The initiated receive sacred garments to remind them of their covenants and the associated spiritual protection. This process is similar to the promised strength that Samson received as part of his Nazarite vows to serve God. The Nazarite covenant came with tokens to remind him that his strength came from God, not his own arm of flesh: he was not to eat vine products, cut his hair, or touch dead bodies (see Numbers 6:1–8). Samson's immoral conduct and his repeated dishonoring of the Nazarite vow and tokens forced God to finally withdraw His protection, leading to Samson's suffering at the hands of Delilah and the Philistines. God expects Latter-day Saints to recognize the sacredness of the covenants they make with Him in His holy house.

The second protection of the endowment is a forewarning of Satan's wiles, techniques, and temptations. Patrons learn about the things that Satan uses most to distract them from seeking God and His kingdom. This forewarning is an empowerment for those who heed it.

These two "castles on a hill," in Manti and Logan, stand as beacons of life and truth to those who seek refuge from evil. They give hope to weary travelers on the journey of life that those who are sanctified through Christ, or those whose "garments [are] washed white through the blood of the Lamb . . . [will enter] into the rest of the Lord their God" (Alma 13:11–12).

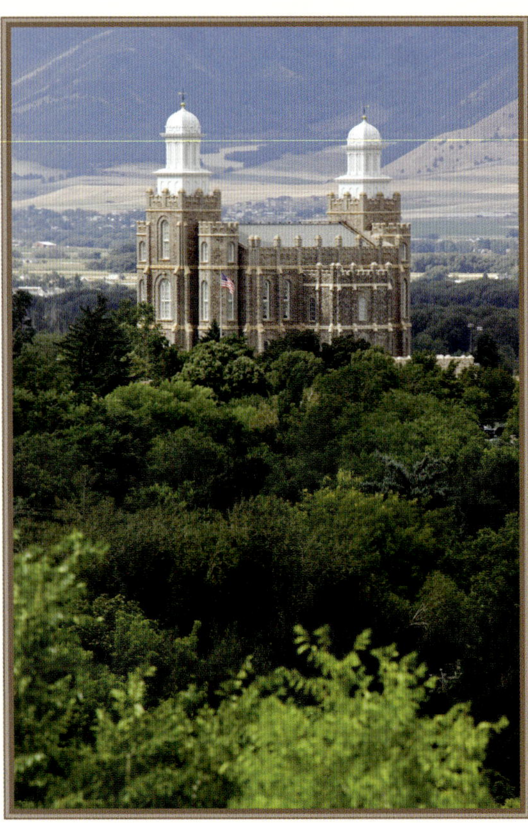

then the great and abominable church took away from it many plain and precious parts as well as many covenants, leading to a spiritual stumbling of many people (see 1 Nephi 13:20–29).

For Latter-day Saints, it is interesting to ponder what was lost to Christianity after the deaths of Christ's Apostles and, therefore, had to be restored through Joseph Smith. It is clear that ethical and moral teachings were not lost after the deaths of the Apostles—almost every Christian and even non-Christian religion throughout history has taught an ethical code that is generally similar to LDS standards of morality. But many doctrinal truths—the plain and precious parts of the gospel—such as the true nature of God, the destiny of man, the three degrees of glory, the premortal existence, the spirit world, and a positive view of the Fall, are absolutely unique to Mormonism. The temple covenants, which lead to even more of the knowledge of God, are equally unique to the restored Church. All of these things were lost and later restored to the earth through Joseph Smith, and the Book of Mormon was integral in that restoration.

Next, Nephi sees that his posterity will write the Book of Mormon and that it will be hidden up to eventually come forth and begin the process of the Restoration (see 1 Nephi 13:35–36). From this great beginning, other books will come forth that will bear witness to the truth of the records of the prophets and Apostles and, significantly, "make known the plain and precious things which have been taken away" (1 Nephi 13:38–40). The Book of Mormon, both by itself and in conjunction with the other works of the Restoration it brought forth, is therefore the key to recognizing, understanding, and counteracting the evils of the great and abominable church.

The implication of this explanation is that we are accountable for making the right choices because we have access to the antidote to the devil's deceptions. Nephi records that if the Gentiles will accept Christ and His teachings, they will be numbered with Israel and be a blessed people. God will do "a marvelous work among the children of men; a work which shall be everlasting," and if they accept it they will be brought unto "peace and life eternal" (1 Nephi 14:7). Since God has done His part by restoring the gospel, His children must do theirs by choosing to live His teachings.

Part four of Nephi's vision reemphasizes this basic choice between good and evil and shows that there are really just these two paths from which to choose. The symbols that the angel uses to portray this are the two churches: the church of the Lamb of God and the church of the devil. Nephi sees that while the choice to live righteously is not normally easy—because wickedness, the whore of all the earth, "[sits] upon many waters; and . . . [has] dominion over all the earth, among all nations, tongues, and people" (1 Nephi 14:11)—it is, nevertheless, possible. In fact, Nephi sees that the power of the Lamb of God descended upon "the saints of the church of the Lamb, and upon the covenant people of the Lord" and that "they were armed with righteousness and with the power of God" (1 Nephi 14:14). He sees that God will eventually destroy wickedness—the great and abominable church—and then begin to fulfill His covenants to the house of Israel. God will judge His children in a final reckoning that will involve both the destruction of the wicked and the blessing of the righteous (see 1 Nephi 14:17).

In analyzing Nephi's vision as a whole, we see that he, like his father, was privileged to see a vision that follows an endowment pattern. First, he received instruction explaining man's eternal journey and destiny by means of stories and figurative representations—the tree and the building, Nephite and Gentile history, and the church of God and the church of the devil. Second, his vision showed him that God provides truths and covenants, through the Book of Mormon and the Restoration, to divinely guide His children on their journey back to His presence. Finally, Nephi learned that there will be an accounting of deeds for the righteous and the wicked, with attendant great blessings for those who chose to serve God, after the judgment and destruction of the church of the devil. Nephi's longer version of the tree of life revelation is obviously an expansion of his father's vision, and it is important to note that the expansion serves to more fully develop the "good/evil contrast" pattern.

This development of and emphasis on the contrast between good and evil may be the most useful aspect of Nephi's vision. It is significantly easier to overcome the enemy of all righteousness when we know his tactics and understand what God has given us as weapons in the war.

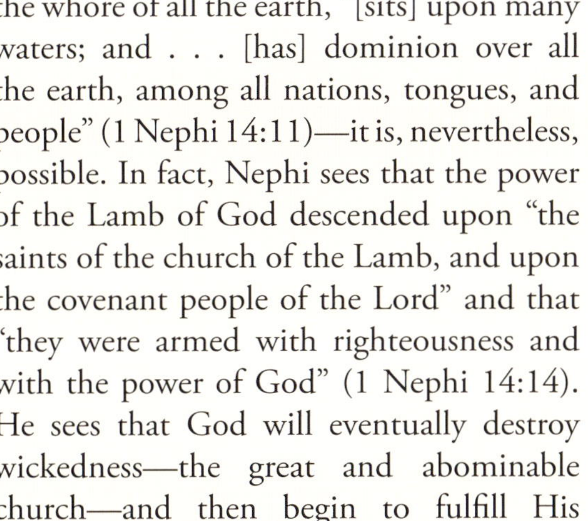

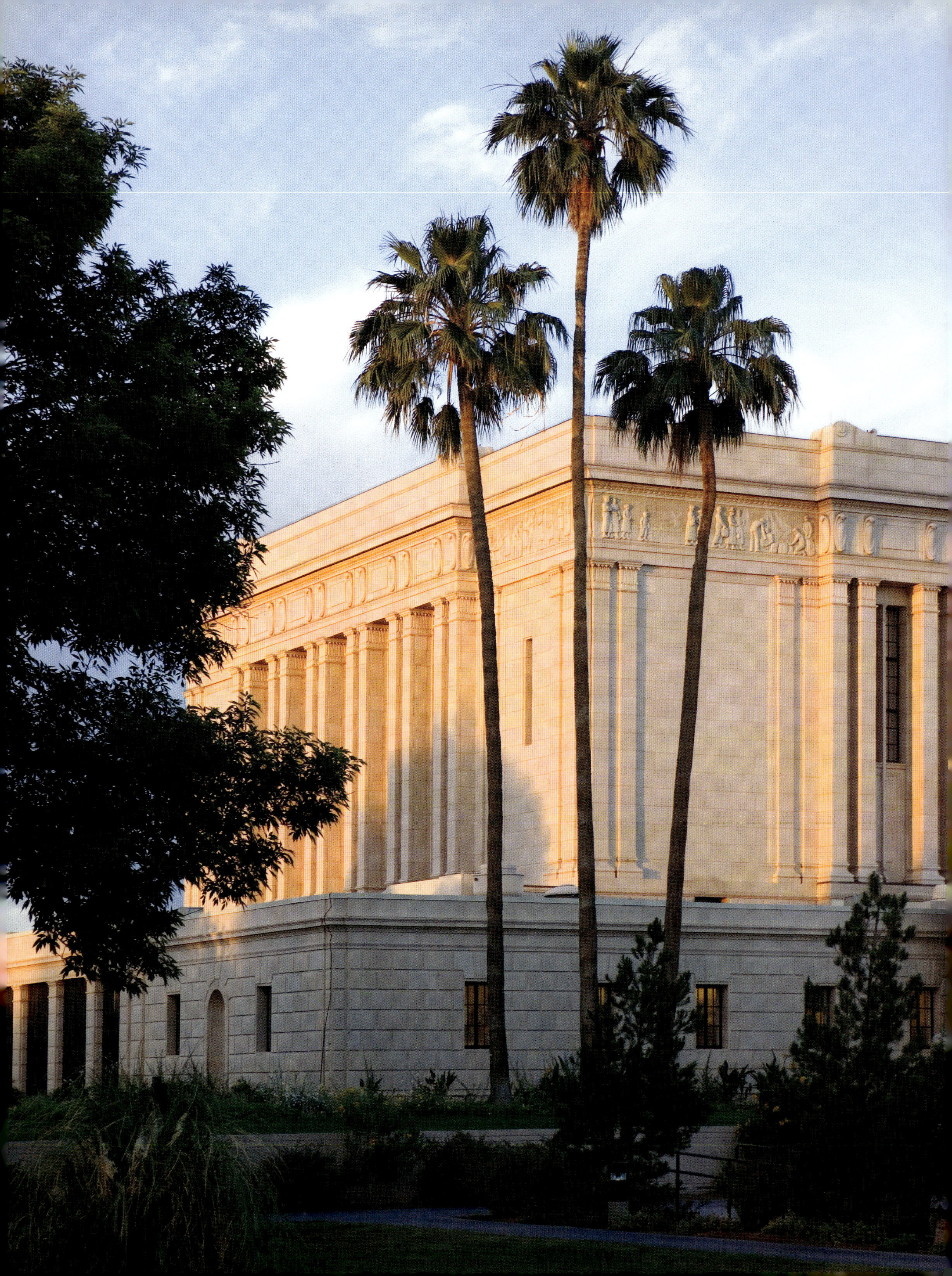

Gathering to the Family of God

1 Nephi 19–22

Why do the Savior, Lehi, Nephi, and Jacob occupy such a large portion of the Book of Mormon with teachings about the doctrine of the gathering? If the main meaning of the gathering is, as is sometimes assumed, that certain peoples will return to certain lands, why dedicate more than two dozen chapters in 1 and 2 Nephi, Jacob, and 3 Nephi to a doctrine that would seem, under that interpretation, to have minor eternal significance? A little reflection on these questions suggests that the doctrine of the gathering has a deeper spiritual significance than God's preference for having certain people live in certain areas—a significance that requires symbolic insight. In its most profound interpretation, the gathering of Israel again leads us to the temple because the ultimate gathering of Israel is to the family of God through temple covenants.

The keys to this gathering by covenant were restored in the Kirtland Temple in 1836 when Moses conferred them upon Joseph Smith (see D&C 110:11). As Joseph Fielding Smith points out, the keys that Moses restored were not the keys to missionary work, as is sometimes taught; that work had already been going on since 1830.[7] Rather, Moses restored the right to administer certain temple ordinances. Joseph Fielding Smith explained:

> The higher ordinances, the greater blessings which are essential to exaltation in the kingdom of God, and which can only be obtained in certain places, no man has a right to perform except as he receives the authority to do it from the one who holds the keys. . . . That is the thing that counts, and that is why Elijah came; that is why Moses came, for he also held keys of the priesthood; . . . that is why they (Moses and Elijah) came to the Prophet Joseph Smith.[8]

With this interpretation in mind, we can better understand that the main reason for God to gather His people at certain times to certain designated places is to facilitate the giving of ordinances. In other words, God gathers a critical mass of converted Saints together in one place to build and staff temples. Joseph Smith taught this principle in these terms:

> What was the object of gathering the Jews, or the people of God in any age of the world? . . . The main object was to build unto the Lord a house whereby He could reveal

> unto His people the ordinances of His house and the glories of His kingdom, and teach the people the way of salvation; for there are certain ordinances and principles that, when they are taught and practiced, must be done in a place or house built for that purpose. . . .
>
> It is for the same purpose that God gathers together His people in the last days, to build unto the Lord a house to prepare them for the ordinances and endowments, washings and anointings, etc.[9]

Thus, God's real reason for gathering His people together in certain areas is not that He likes certain properties or dislikes cultural diversity. The literal gathering to specific lands is mostly to facilitate the spiritual gathering—a gathering to Heavenly Father's family through the reception of temple covenants. In this dispensation the Saints have gathered to Ohio and Missouri, then Illinois, then Utah, and currently to the stakes of Zion. No matter where the Saints relocated, almost the first thing they did upon arrival was lay the cornerstones for the temple they intended to build at the center of their community. In our generation, President Gordon B. Hinckley made it possible, with his expanded temple-building program, for Latter-day Saints to "gather" to God's family in many, many places on the earth. *Where* the gathering takes place is less important than *why.* In other words, as Elder Russell M. Nelson taught concerning the modern Church, which has temples dotting the earth, "The choice to come unto Christ is not a matter of physical location; it is a matter of individual commitment. People can be 'brought to the knowledge of the Lord' without leaving their homelands."[10]

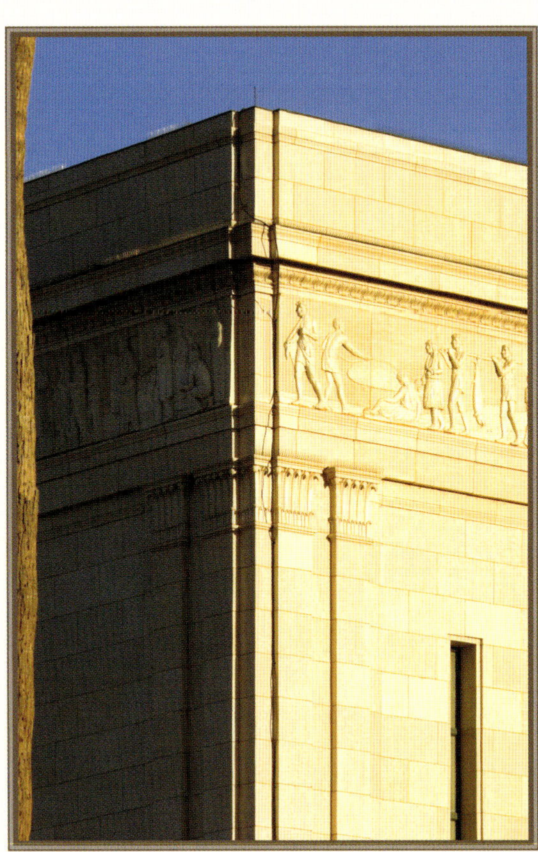

In the Book of Mormon, the doctrine of gathering is most often taught in association with long quotations of Isaiah accompanied by commentary. This quotation/commentary pattern first occurs in the last four chapters of 1 Nephi, where Nephi gives prophetic insight on Isaiah both before and after the two chapters of quotation. In his introductory remarks (1 Nephi 19), Nephi gives three clues on how to read what he quotes from Isaiah. First, he declares that he will write only what he thinks is sacred (see 1 Nephi 19:6–7). Second, he recounts a short history of the rejection and crucifixion of Christ by His own people with the promise that when they eventually accept Him as the Holy One of Israel, God will gather them (see 1 Nephi 19:15–16). And third, he declares that he is going to quote from Isaiah in order to more fully persuade his people to remember the Lord and that he wants his listeners to liken his words unto their lives (see 1 Nephi 19:8–21). In short, the three keys to deciphering the Isaiah quotes and Nephi's commentary are, first, his writings are sacred; second, the central message is acceptance of Christ; and third, the Isaiah quotations must be likened to ourselves, meaning that the principles taught should be applied figuratively by each individual reader.

Of the three, the last may be the most important, since most of the information in Isaiah is historical or poetically symbolic and not terribly important in and of itself in today's world. Unless Isaiah is likened to our own circumstances today, much of it seems irrelevant. For instance, why does the prophet admonish readers to "Go ye forth of Babylon" (1 Nephi 20:20), a country that ceased to exist in the sixth century BC, unless that counsel somehow has spiritual application to modern readers—unless it is a metaphor for repentance? Likewise, are we to believe that Christ literally complains that His labors are in vain? (See 1 Nephi 21:4.) Or rather, should we understand that this poetic invention sets up the later point that Christ's Atonement will eventually triumph and that He will save both Israel and the Gentiles (see 1 Nephi 21:6)—a teaching that encourages the righteous to endure to the end? In terms of logic, it makes little sense to waste precious space on gold plates—dedicated to spiritual concerns—on subject matter that deals mostly with distant times and peoples unless it teaches crucial principles that can be applied to our lives.

With this likening principle in mind, the second key to reading Isaiah—the central message is acceptance of Christ—makes perfect sense. When applied to our day, the theme of scattering and gathering—so pervasively present in Isaiah's

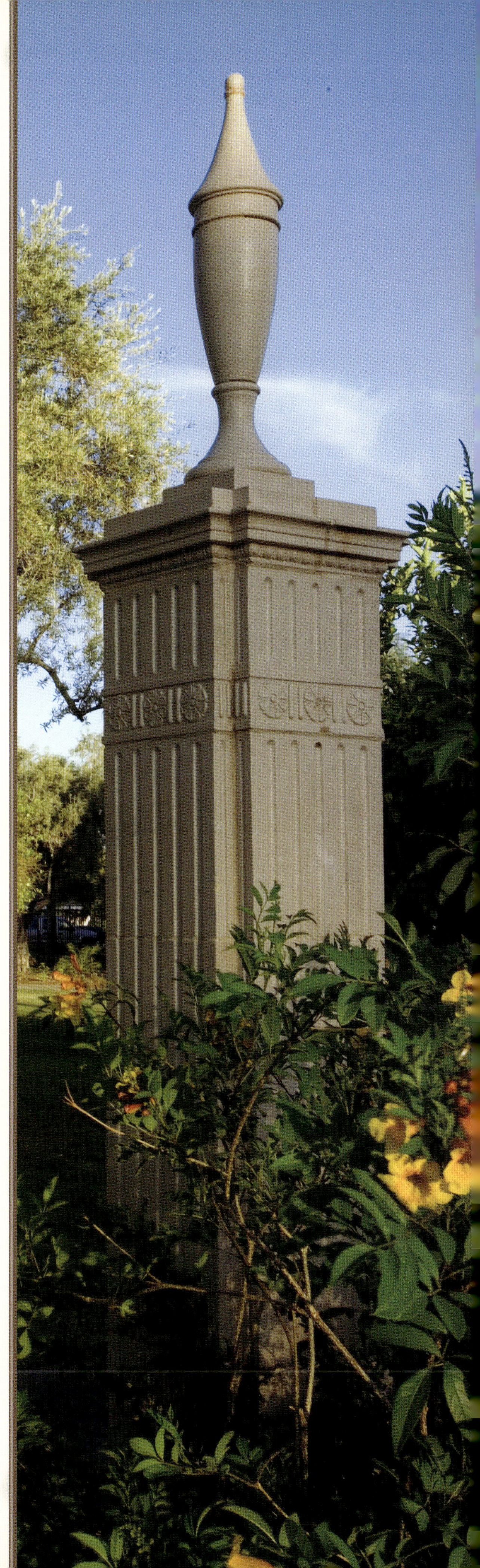

Mesa Arizona Temple

Gathering to the Family of God

The Mesa Arizona Temple portrays the gathering of Israel more than any other temple in the Church. Clearly visible from the surrounding gardens and lawn are eight friezes on the corners of the temple portraying many peoples from different cultures gathering to be with the Saints.

The eight friezes portray:

1. The gathering of the Saints to the Rocky Mountains
2. The English and Welsh boarding a ship as they prepare to gather to Zion
3. Latter-day Saints traveling by handcart
4. Mexican Saints
5. Native Americans
6. Pacific Islanders
7. French and Swiss Saints
8. German and Dutch Saints

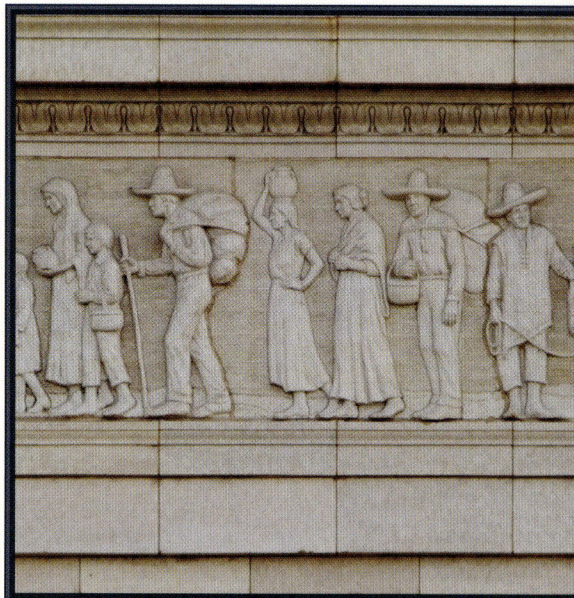

The physical gathering depicted in the friezes is a symbol of the most important gathering: the spiritual gathering to the family of God that occurs when Latter-day Saints receive and keep their temple covenants. Elder George A. Smith explains this principle in these terms:

"Among the first principles that were revealed to the children of men in the last days was the gathering; the first revelations that were given to the Church were to command them to gather, and send Elders to seek out a place for the gathering of the Saints. What is the gathering for? Why was it that the Savior wished the children of Israel to gather together? It was that they might become united and provide a place wherein he could reveal unto them keys which have been hid before the foundation of the world; that he could unfold unto them the laws of exaltation, and make them a kingdom of Priests, even the whole people, and exalt them to thrones and dominions in the celestial world."[11]

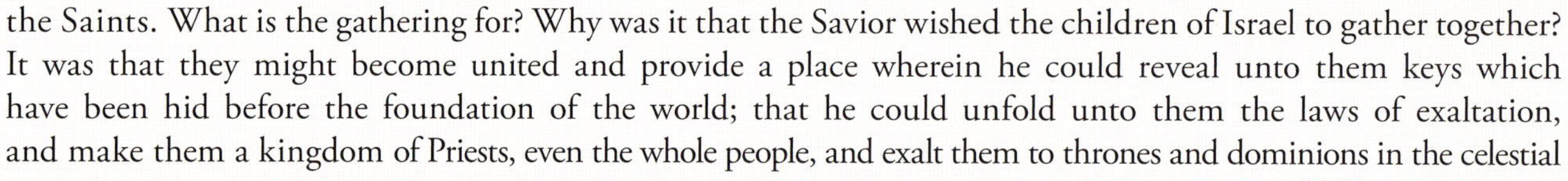

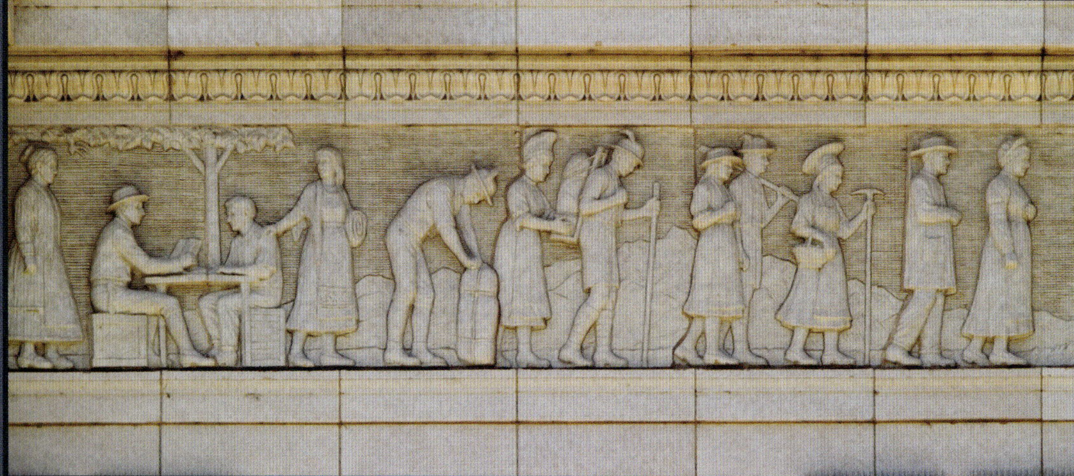

In peaceful temples, like this one in the desert of Arizona, God's people receive the keys necessary to exalt them. By this means they gather eternally to God's family.

writings—becomes a symbol of the power of the Atonement. The literal scattering of Israel that Isaiah describes in 1 Nephi 20 is symbolic of how we, in modern times, distance ourselves from God's help and inspiration when we willfully sin. The literal gathering of Israel that he describes in 1 Nephi 21 is symbolic of gathering back to God through repentance and the Atonement and by covenant.[12] Isaiah's writings thus can be understood both literally and figuratively, or, as Nephi himself says, both temporally and spiritually (see 1 Nephi 22:3), but it is the figurative application that is most vital to spiritual understanding. Thus Nephi's approach is to quote Isaiah passages, explain their principles, and expect his readers to apply to themselves the principles of repentance and keeping covenants. Collectively, God's people apply the principle of gathering by gathering to certain locations, building temples, and receiving covenants. Individually, and most importantly, we apply the gathering by repenting, coming back to God, accepting Christ's Atonement, and making covenants. In other words, the gathering is first and foremost about accepting the Atonement and the covenants.

Not only does Nephi predispose us to this interpretation in his introduction to his Isaiah quotation, but he also emphasizes it in his concluding commentary in 1 Nephi 22. He witnesses that the people of Israel will be literally scattered because they will harden their hearts against Christ, the hardened heart symbolizing that they have already spiritually "scattered" themselves from God

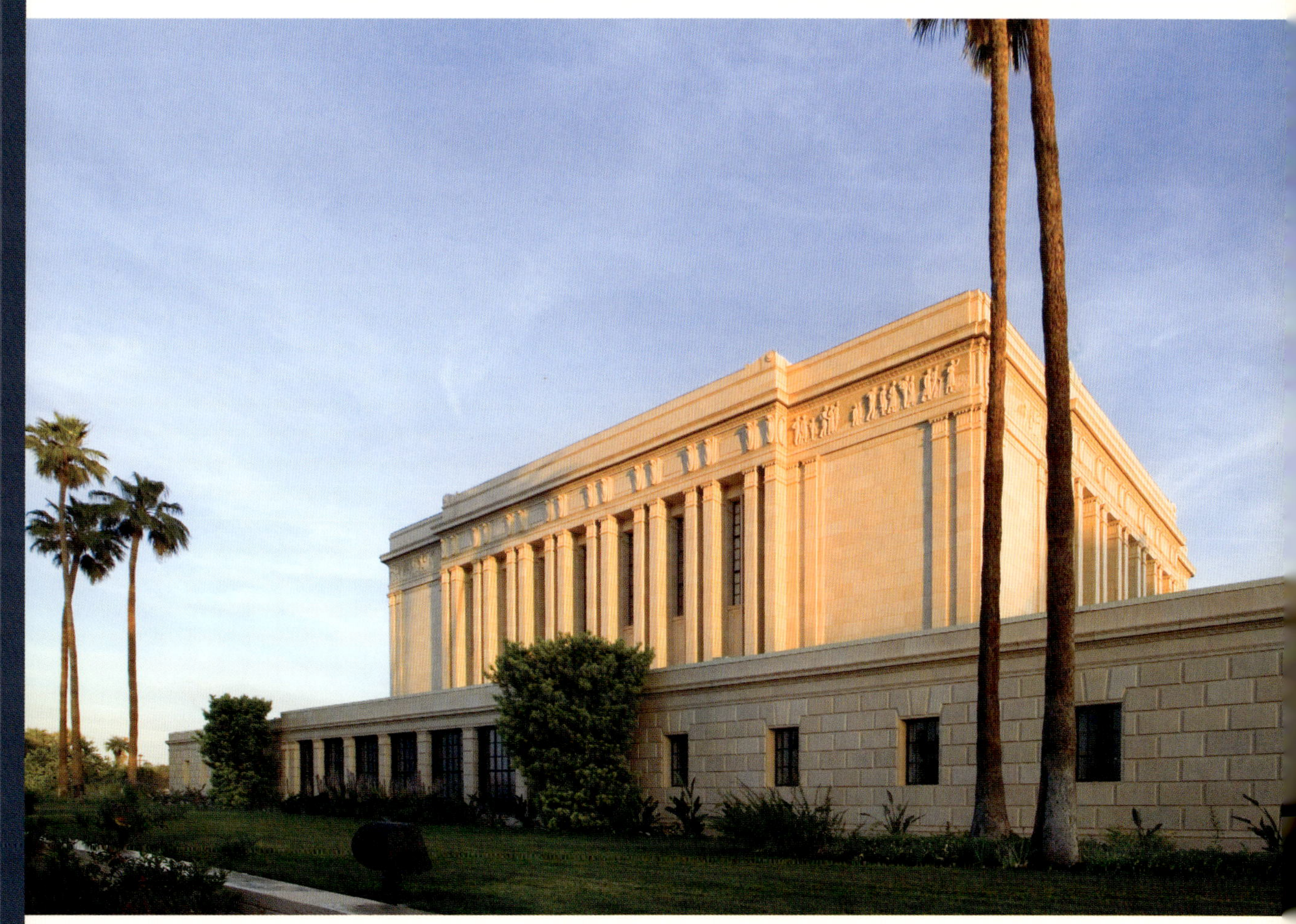

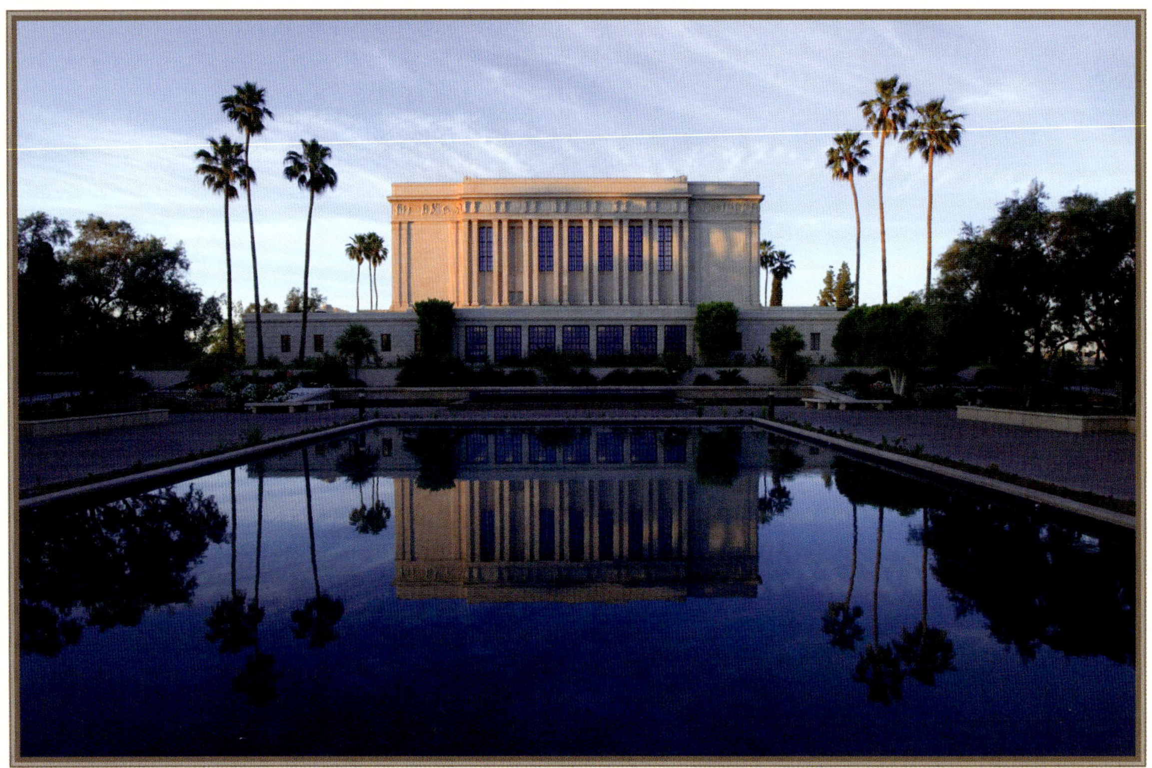

(see 1 Nephi 22:3–5). Nephi further explains that God will do a "marvelous work among the Gentiles, which shall be of great worth" to Lehi's descendents and to the Gentiles and to all of Israel (1 Nephi 22:6–9). Nephi says that this great work will be literal (see 1 Nephi 22:6), but it is figuratively represented by Isaiah as having the Gentiles nurse Israel and carry Israel on their shoulders and in their arms (see 1 Nephi 22:6–8). Latter-day Saints, who are mostly Gentiles by nationality (though not by covenant or lineage), understand this marvelous work as the gathering of scattered Israel to the gospel fold through the Restoration of the gospel of Christ, and its spread throughout the earth by missionary and temple work. It is not secular rulers but rather priesthood kings and queens, offering temple covenants to honest-hearted converts, who are the nursing fathers and mothers. This interpretation makes the discussion far more personal and applicable than the political gathering of the Jewish people.

In contrast to those who will be gathered to the fold of God through their acceptance of Christ's Atonement and the covenants that lead to exaltation, Nephi also explains the final outcome of those who deny Christ and His Atonement. He shows that the wicked, symbolized by the abominable church and the whore of the earth, will be scattered and destroyed as they turn on each other and war against each other and then are burned (see 1 Nephi 22:13–15). This awful fate seems even more dire when juxtaposed with the blessing and final triumph of the righteous, which Nephi figuratively portrays as God gathering His sheep and finding them pasture (see 1 Nephi 22:24–25).

Isaiah thus teaches literally and figuratively that God will protect the righteous, destroy the wicked, and establish peace during the millennium for those who have repented (see 1 Nephi 22:16–28). And Nephi expects his readers to apply these principles to themselves as a call to gather to God's family by personal repentance and temple covenant.

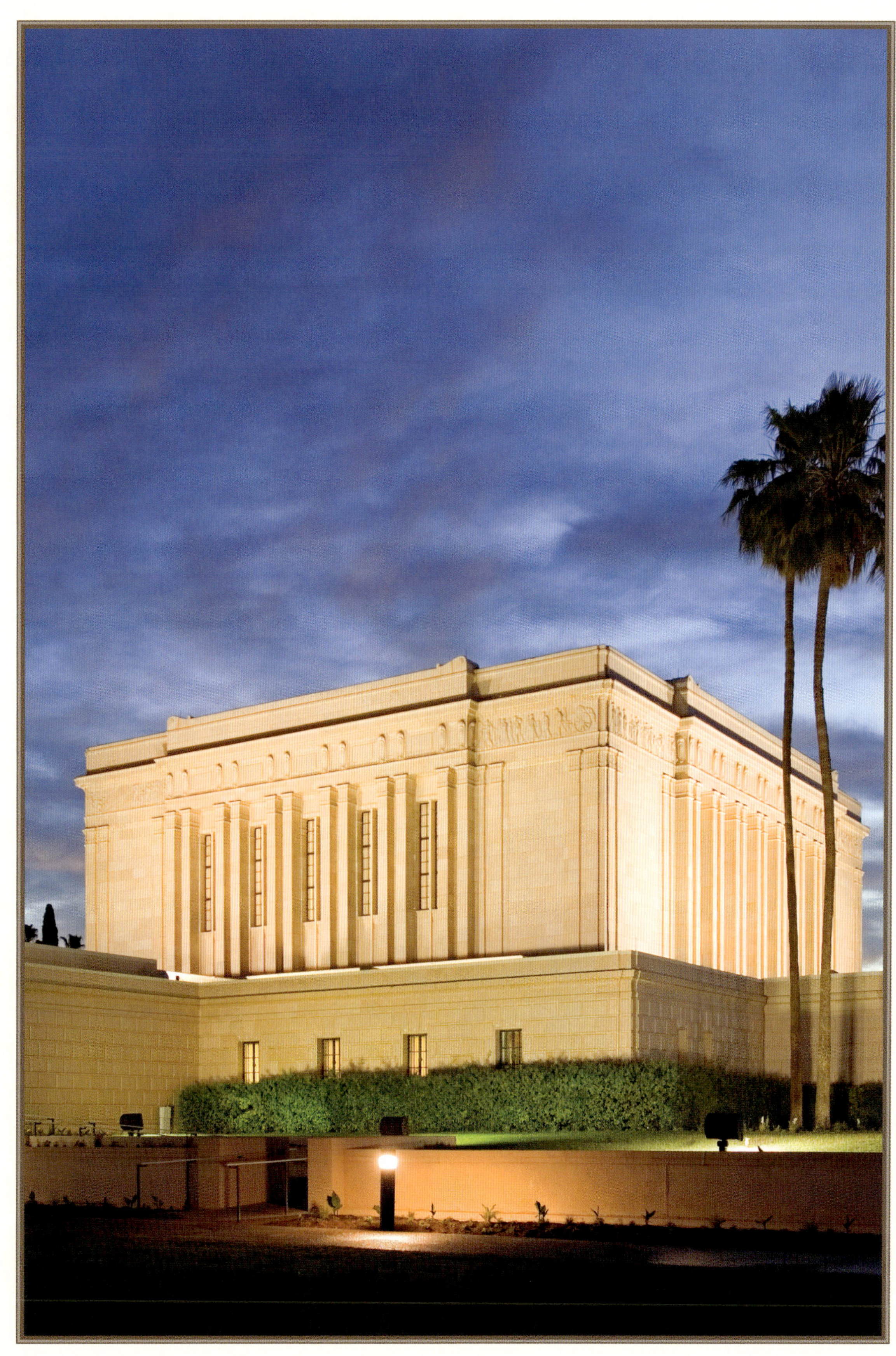

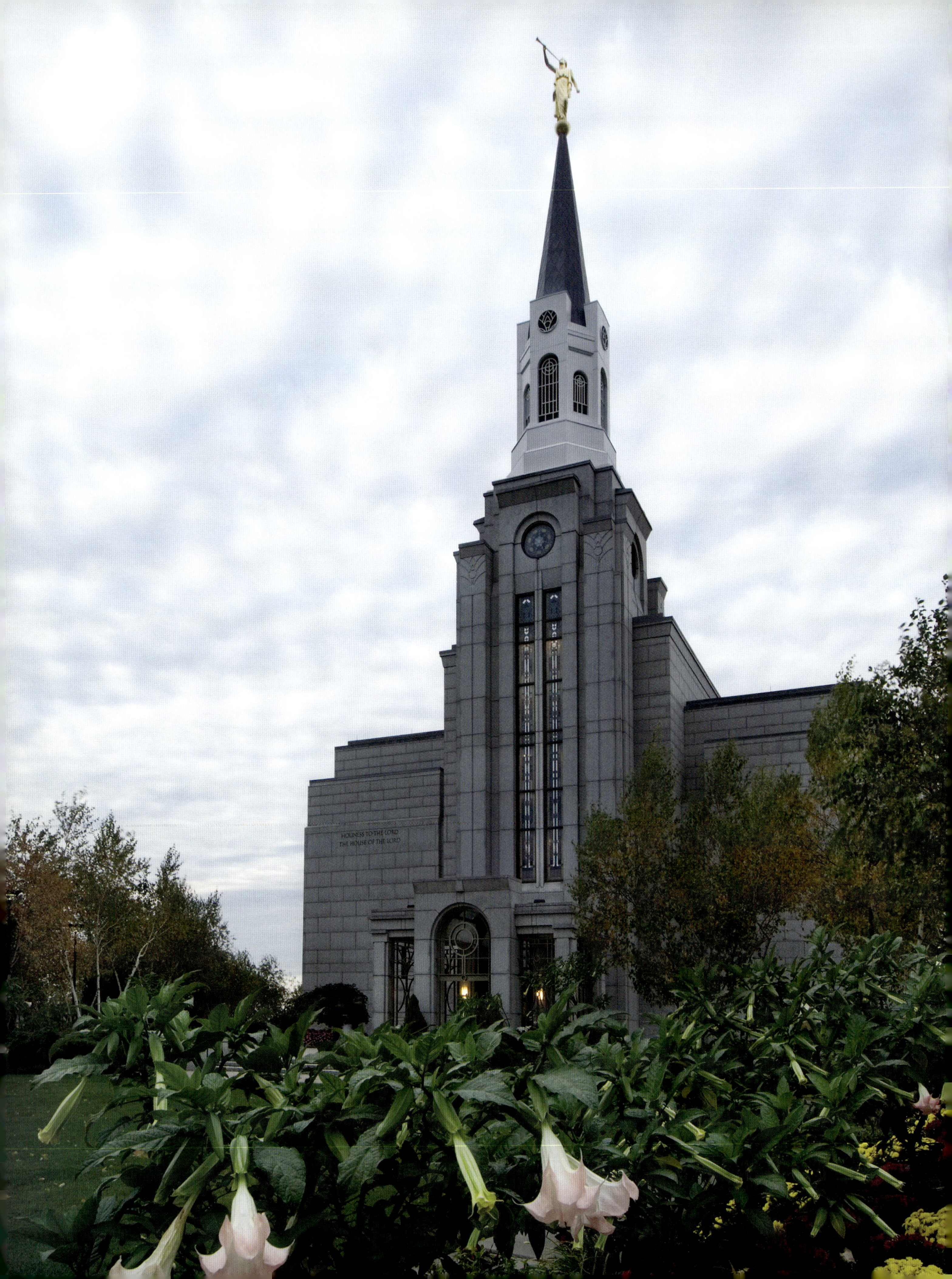
HOLINESS TO THE LORD
THE HOUSE OF THE LORD

Returning to the Tree of Life

2 Nephi 2

The endowment empowers Latter-day Saints to return to the presence of God, which is symbolized in the scriptures by the tree of life. The endowment's symbolic instruction explains how the Fall initiated the test of mortality and how the Atonement enables men and women to pass this test. It does this by clarifying the fallen conditions experienced by mortal human beings and by explaining the conditions and covenants that every person must meet and keep to make the Atonement fully effective in his or her life. The Fall and the Atonement are the center and the circumference of the endowment ceremony. Each helps us understand the other, and together they show the path to the tree of life, or exaltation. As President Ezra Taft Benson taught, if we miss the relationship between the Fall and the Atonement we cannot really understand the need for a Savior: "No one adequately knows why he needs Christ until he understands and accepts the doctrine of the Fall and its effect upon all mankind."[13] Lehi apparently understood this crucial principle and connection. It is for this reason that he explained the connection between the Fall and the Atonement in one of the last sermons he gave to his sons[14] before his death (see 2 Nephi 2) and then admonished them to choose the Atonement. It is also for this reason that we will examine the Fall in this chapter and then show how Lehi used this doctrine in exhorting his sons to repent.

While most of Christianity knows there would not have been an Atonement if there had not been a Fall, Latter-day Saints are quite unique in believing that the Fall was a good thing, that it was foreordained, and that it is absolutely essential to the plan of exaltation (see 2 Nephi 2:25). Elder Bruce R. McConkie even went so far as to call it one of the three pillars of eternity.[15] This unusually positive view of the Fall makes much more sense than the traditional negative view, particularly in light of Adam and Eve's own affirmative response to their fall (see Moses 5:10–11) as well as Lehi's explanation that the Fall brought about God's eternal purposes, the existence of humankind, and the chance to do good in mortality (see 2 Nephi 2:15, 23).

Doctrinally, most Latter-day Saints agree that the Fall was an integral part of the plan and, therefore, a good thing. But confusion creeps in for many when they read the account of the Fall in Genesis 2–3 (or even in Moses 3–4),[16] which appears to negatively show Adam and Eve disobeying the commands of God. The seeming discrepancy between the positive doctrine and the negative account raises difficult and confusing questions, such as *How could Adam and Eve obey and disobey at the same time?* and *Why would God forbid Adam and Eve to do the very thing*

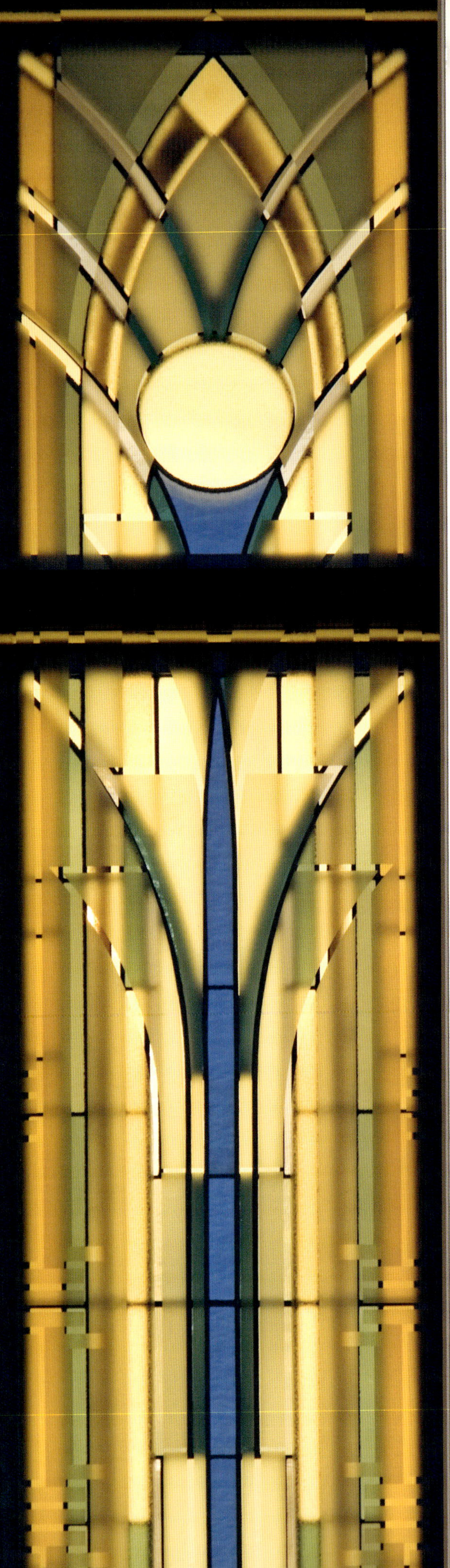

that they were foreordained to do? Some have suggested that God gave a higher and a lesser commandment so that Adam and Eve had to break one to keep the other. The problem with this explanation is that it is hard to have faith in a God who sets His children up to fail and then punishes them for doing so. In fact, it is out of God's character to act in such a manner. Others have speculated that Adam and Eve should have waited for further instruction, making the issue a question of timing. But there is no way to know if such a hypothesis is really true—the story gives no such indication. Read as pure history, the Fall is puzzling and confusing.

However, read through the "likening" eyes that Nephi talked about (see 1 Nephi 19:23–24), the story of the Fall allows readers to "see" an explanation of the mortal condition and the need for the Atonement. The story is meant to be read mostly as a symbolic exposition, not primarily as a literal, historical account. This does not suggest that Adam and Eve weren't real people, but it does suggest that the account is not Adam's journal entry, but rather a presentation—like the figurative course of instruction in the temple—of the destiny of man, the temptations of Satan, our relationship to God, and our absolute need for a Savior. The account may have literal elements in it, but focusing on that aspect of the story would be missing the point. Indeed, most of the confusion about the doctrine of the Fall has resulted from an insistence on a literal reading. To better understand the doctrine of the Fall, and to understand why Lehi would use it to teach his sons about agency, we will study the figurative meanings of the account. To do so, we will examine several of the symbolic elements of the Fall as recorded in the book of Moses, chapters 3 and 4, knowing that Lehi himself used a similar scriptural record as the basis for his sermon (see 2 Nephi 2:17).

The Rib

The creation of woman out of Adam's rib represents the nature of the relationship between a husband and a wife in eternal marriage. It symbolizes that a man is not eternally complete without a woman. She is part of his life and his eternity. They are to walk side by side throughout life and be one flesh, a phrase that has both physical and spiritual meanings.

This symbol beautifully and poetically teaches the doctrine that men and women cannot be exalted without each other. Temple marriage opens the door to exaltation, and it requires both a man and a woman working together as the most appropriate help for each other to achieve eternal life. Even the language of the account teaches this concept.

The phrase *help meet* means "help most appropriate." Unfortunately, this meaning is often lost because "help meet" regularly gets used as a compound noun, as in the sentence, "She is my help meet." In reality, the phrase is composed of the noun *help* and the adjective *meet,* meaning "appropriate or best."[17] In other words, the language emphasizes that no other living thing can take the place of a righteous spouse. Husbands must help wives and wives must help husbands obtain exaltation. They are to be one in purpose as they strive to become like Heavenly Father. This is the purpose of the plan and the reason God instituted it—that husband and wife together may obtain exaltation.

The Trees and the Forbidden Fruit

In a figurative reading, the forbidden fruit can be read on at least two levels: one that helps explain the doctrine of the Fall and one that warns men and women that there are consequences for disobedience to God. On the first level, the figurative reading symbolizes choices for Adam and Eve. Elder Bruce R.

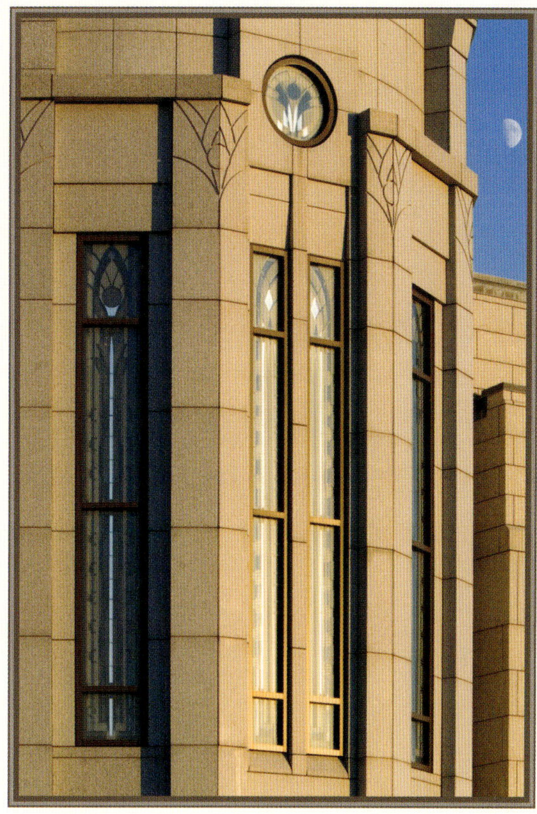

McConkie suggests that for them the tree of knowledge of good and evil—and thus the forbidden fruit—symbolizes the choice to become mortal:

> As to the Fall itself we are told that the Lord planted "the tree of knowledge of good and evil" in the midst of the garden (Moses 3:9). To Adam and Eve the command came: "Of every tree of the garden thou mayest freely eat, But of the tree of knowledge of good and evil, thou shalt not eat of it, nevertheless, thou mayest choose for thyself, for it is given unto thee; but, remember that I forbid it, for in the day thou eatest thereof thou shalt surely die" (Moses 3:16–17). Again the account is speaking figuratively. What is meant by partaking of the fruit of the knowledge of good and evil is that our first parents complied with whatever laws were involved so that their bodies would change from their state of paradisiacal immortality to a state of natural mortality.[18]

The doctrine of the Fall begins, according to Lehi, with the understanding that "Adam fell that men might be; and men are, that they might have joy" (2 Nephi 2:25). God gave Adam the choice to stay in the garden or to leave, and, as President Kimball said, Adam "intentionally and wisely partook of the forbidden fruit."[19] He knowingly and righteously and literally fell so that the mortal test might begin. Adam and Eve made the choice that caused their bodies to change so that they and their future children could experience mortality. It was not wrong, nor a mistake, but exactly what God expected of them. One of the best teachings ever on this principle was provided by President Joseph Fielding Smith:

> . . . It wasn't a shameful fall. What did Adam do? The very thing the Lord wanted him to do, and I hate to hear anybody call it a sin, for it wasn't a sin. Did Adam sin when he partook of the forbidden fruit? I say to you, no, he did not! Now, let me refer to what is written in the Book of Moses in regard to this commandment which the Lord gave to Adam.
>
> "And I, the Lord God, commanded the man, saying: Of every tree of the garden thou mayest freely eat, But of the tree of the knowledge of good and evil, thou shalt not eat of it, nevertheless, thou mayest choose for thyself, for it is given unto thee; but, remember that I forbid it, for in the day thou eatest thereof thou shalt surely die" [Moses 3:16–17].
>
> Now this is the way I interpret that. The Lord said to Adam, here is the tree of the knowledge of good and evil. If you want to stay here then you cannot eat of that fruit. If you want to stay here I forbid you to eat it. But you may act for yourself and you may eat of it if you want to. And if you eat it you will die.
>
> I see a great difference between transgressing the law and committing

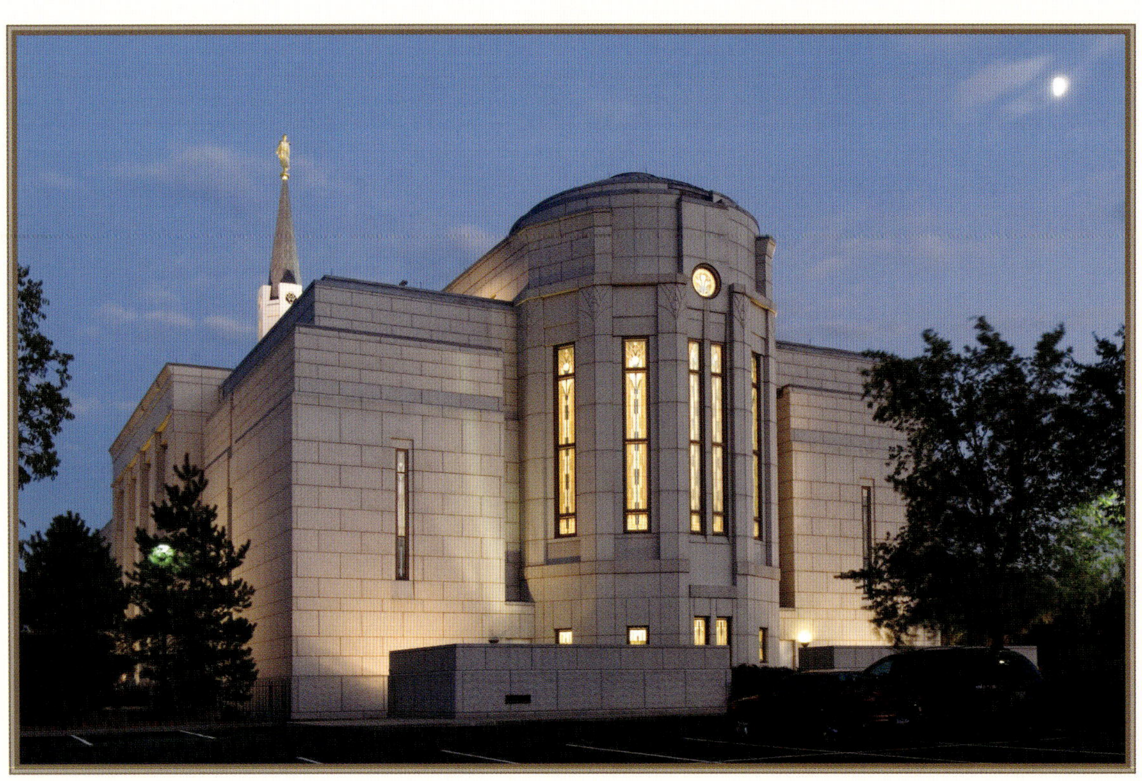

a sin. I have used the illustration that water is composed of two elements. When separate either of them will burn. When brought together they form water which won't burn. A chemist, then, if he joins the two gases together, transgresses a law, doesn't he? Just as Adam did, but he hasn't committed a sin.[20]

According to this insight by President Joseph Fielding Smith, Adam and Eve's "transgression" simply meant that they crossed over from immortality to mortality. For most of humanity, the term *transgression* generally carries a more negative connotation implying sin, but not for Adam and Eve in the garden. *Webster's* dictionary says that *transgress* can also mean "to step beyond or across; to go beyond limits set."[21] The term *transgress* by this definition means "to cross over," just as progress means to go forward, regress means to go backward, and digress means to go to the side. Adam and Eve thus *transgressed,* or crossed over to mortality just as God wanted, so that the test of life could start.

On the second level, the figurative reading symbolizes choices for each mortal individual who has come to earth. The tree of life represents obedience to God's teachings, and the tree of knowledge of good and evil represents disobedience. The negative-sounding injunction "I forbid it" should be read as a metaphor for forbidding sin to human beings. The significant addition in the Pearl of Great Price of the phrase "thou mayest choose for thyself, for it is given unto thee" (Moses 3:17) supports this figurative reading of the story. It makes no sense in a literal reading for God to forbid Adam and Eve to eat of the tree and then tell them that they can if they want to. What would be the purpose of such a literal command? On the figurative level, however, it teaches the doctrine of agency—that mortal men and women *should*

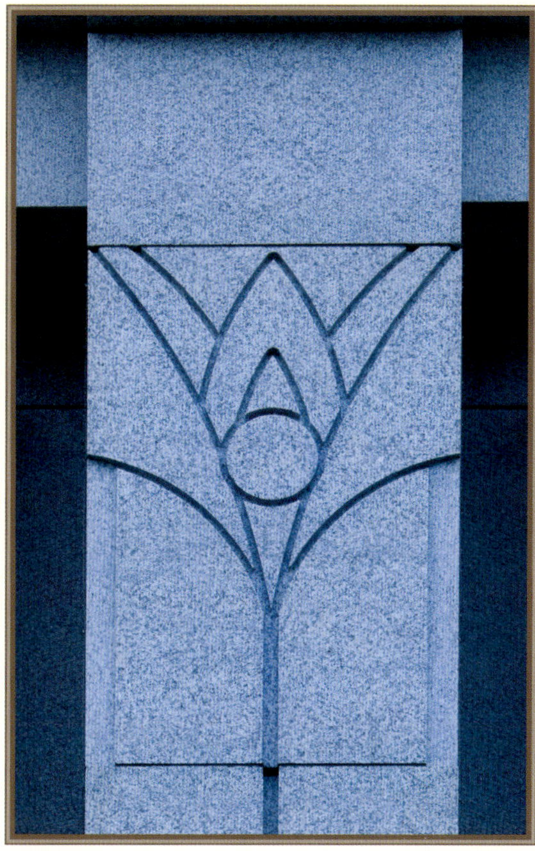

be obedient to God, but they have the agency to reject His teachings if they choose. Read on this level, the story becomes a presentation of the universal mortal condition and the need for the Atonement.

The Serpent

The serpent in the story symbolizes the way that Satan tempts us through other people and the fact that the temptations are generally snakelike—sly, devious, and subtle. The serpent tempts Eve by trying to convince her that God has restricted her. He tells her that she can't eat from all the trees. This is the same type of argument that Latter-day Saints face from tempters who tell them they do not really understand life because they "cannot" enjoy the "pleasures" of sin, that they are too restricted by commandments.

In the story, Eve responds that the serpent's words are not true. She says that God did

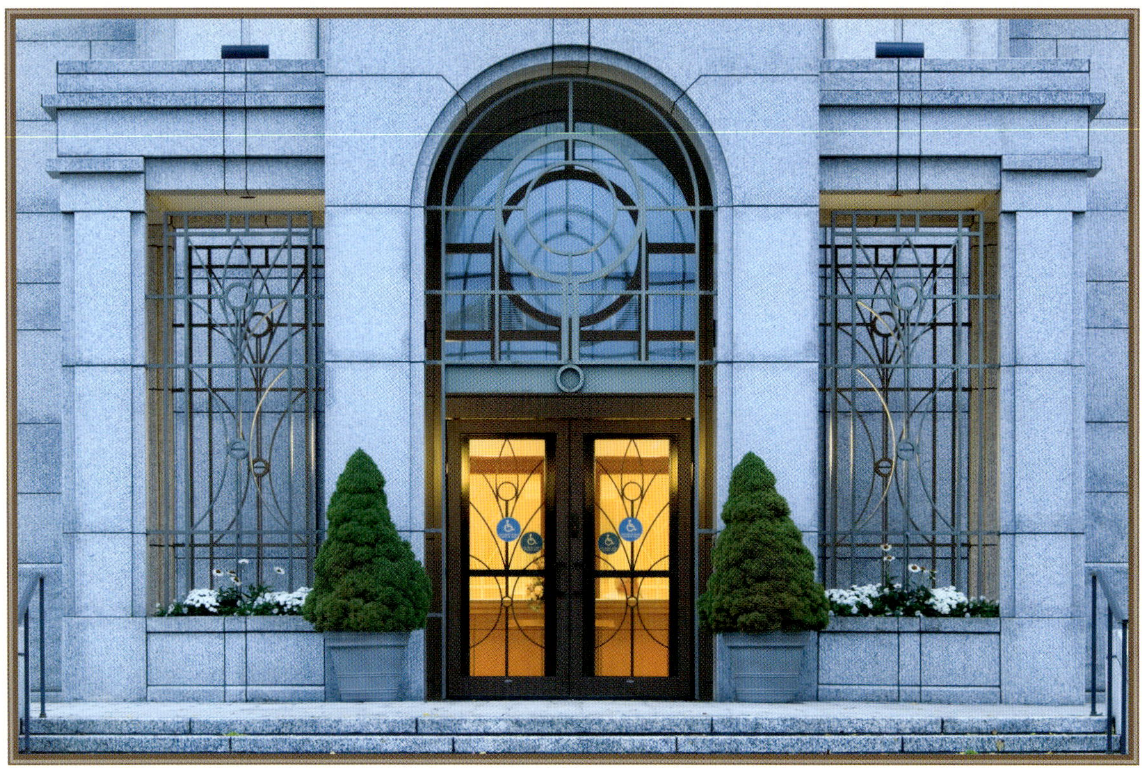

not say she could not eat from the tree, only that there would be consequences if she did, symbolizing for Latter-day Saints that they do, indeed, have the agency to break God's commandments but must always face consequences for so doing.

Satan responds with the half-truth that there will not be consequences but that Eve will become like a god, knowing good and evil. Modern tempters employ similar types of propaganda when they insinuate that sin allows them to understand life better, experience all things, and have insights unknown to the obedient.

In the story, Eve succumbs to the temptation for a variety of reasons: it is good for food, pleasant to look at, and desired to make her wise. She partakes of the fruit and then convinces her husband to join her in the disobedience. On the symbolic level, this illustrates the truth that those who succumb to temptation are often convinced of the inherent rightness of all pleasure and that there will be no consequences to disobedience. They find reasons to justify their actions, and they often drag others into their errant ways.

The temptation of Eve teaches God's children how Satan seeks to destroy their agency. He cannot do it by force—not even God can do that—so he limits their options by lies, half-truths, and various other propaganda techniques. He knows that if people do not know what the real truth is, they cannot choose to follow it. They may get lucky and choose truth by chance, without the real use of their agency, but much of the time they will not be so fortunate. If Satan can make mortals choose errantly, he can, at the very least, lead them into unhappy consequences that will unnecessarily complicate their lives. Even worse, he can often deceive them into making choices that can become addicting and further limit agency or ruin their mortal probation. He is "the father of all lies," and his goal is "to deceive and to blind men, and to lead them captive at his will" (Moses 4:4). Ignorance of truth is his best weapon.

Boston Massachusetts Temple

Returning to the Tree of Life

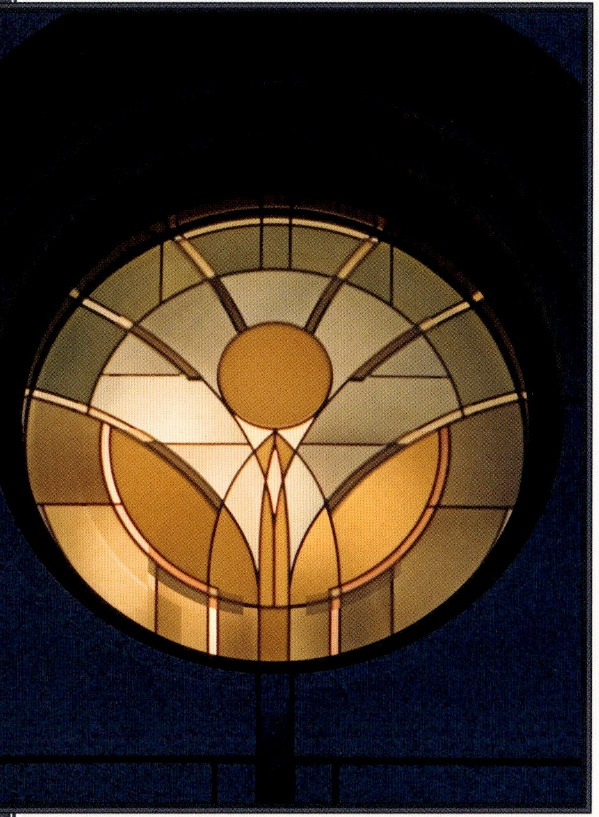

No matter where you walk at the Boston Massachusetts Temple, you encounter the symbol of the tree of life in stylized form. The thin line that represents the tree trunk, topped by a flowerlike figure representing the leafy portion of the tree, is seen on the top of the pilasters on the front of the temple, on the back of the temple, and on the sides. It is seen in the widows as well, and in the middle of the battlements on the central tower.

The message of this ubiquitous tree is that this place, the house of the Lord, is the means by which men and women can pass the guardian cherubim and partake of the tree of life. Or, as stated by the Third Article of Faith: "We believe that through the Atonement of Christ, all mankind may be saved, by obedience to the laws and ordinances of the Gospel" (Articles of Faith 1:3). It is the laws and ordinances, especially the laws of the baptismal and temple covenants, that must be obeyed for the Atonement to take full effect and lead to exaltation. This is the means that God has given to His children to help them overcome their fallen nature.

The tree of life is the great symbol of the healing powers of the Atonement (see Revelation 22:1–2). It is also the most common symbol associated with the story of the Fall. And finally, it is the symbol of the love of God, which all people can experience if they will just follow the path that will carry them to God's presence.

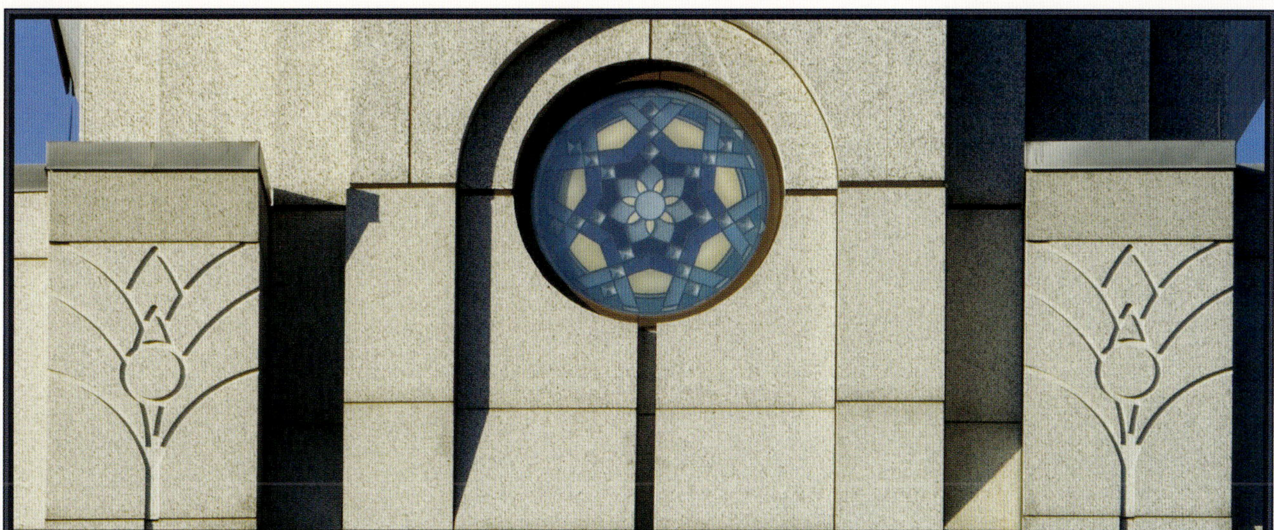

The Aprons

In the story, Adam and Eve make aprons to cover their nakedness, which represents their guilt. This is a fairly typical reaction. It is not unusual for the guilty to seek to hide their sins. But if one cannot admit sin, there is no motivation or room to repent. Thus God has said, "By this ye may know if a man repenteth of his sins—behold, he will confess them and forsake them" (D&C 58:43). This may be what God is trying to get Adam to do in the "bishop's interview" in Moses 4:15–19, when God asks Adam where he is going and what he has done. Instead of taking full responsibility for his own actions, however, Adam responds by blaming Eve. Eve responds to the same question by blaming the serpent. On the symbolic level, this part of the story should convict those who never self-examine and who normally deny their need for change and the Atonement.

This part of the story should, thus, cause every mortal human being to pause and question how much self-justification exists in his or her own life, how much he or she hides sins or unrighteously blames others. It should also cause us to recognize that since "all have sinned, and come short of the glory of God" (Romans 3:23), everyone has absolute need of a Savior. It is at this point in the story, the cursing of the serpent, that the promise of a Savior is given.

The Cursing of the Serpent

A literal reading of the account has God talking to and taking away the legs of a skinny animal known as the serpent because it tempted Eve. A figurative reading yields much deeper insight. First, it shows that Satan does not have power over human beings unless they grant that power by their own choices. Just as men and women can normally avoid snakes—an animal without legs—or run to get away from them if they want to, so can they stay out of Satan's power if they so choose. If they get bitten by a snake, or Satan, it is probably because they got too close.

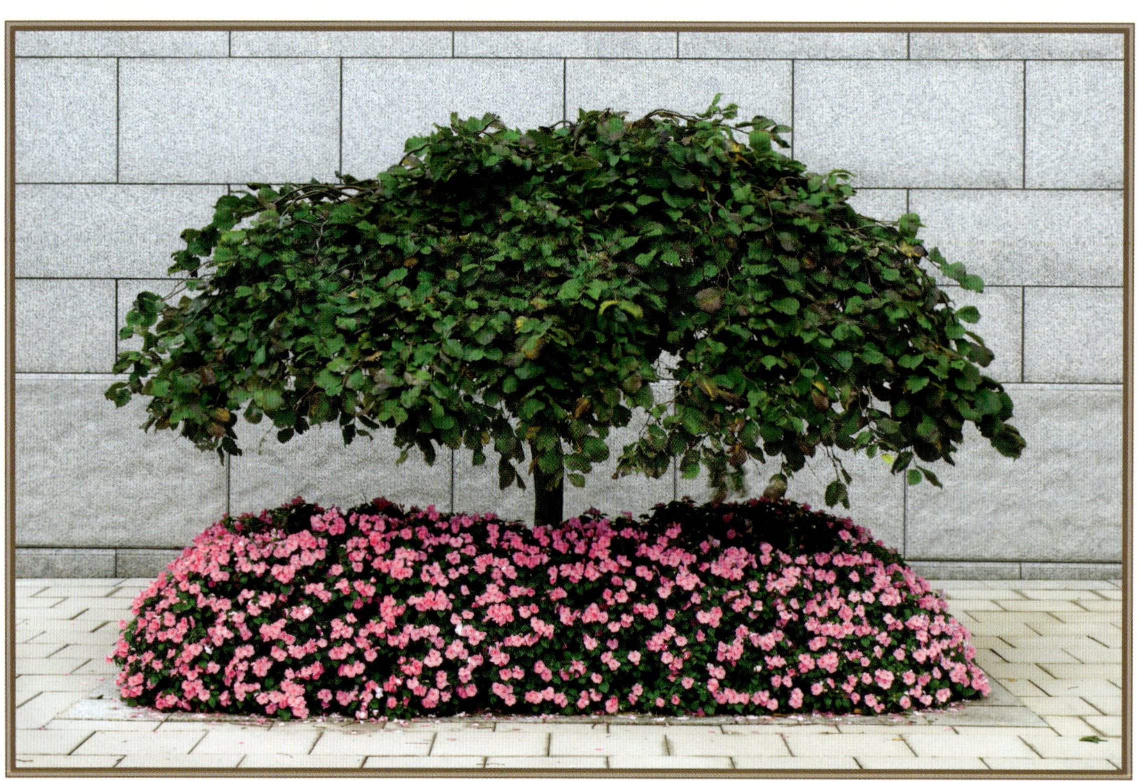

Second, a figurative reading renders the cursing of the serpent as the promise of a Savior. God tells the serpent, which Lehi identifies as Satan (see 2 Nephi 2:18), that he will be allowed to bruise the heel of Eve's posterity, presumably in the way described above—by deception, sin, and spiritual captivity. But God also promises that Eve's posterity—in this case, Jesus Christ—will bruise the head of the serpent (see Moses 4:21). A bruised heel is painful but not normally deadly. A bruised head, on the other hand, is most likely fatal. Thus, when seen figuratively, the curse of the serpent promises God's children that His power is greater than Satan's.

Instructions to Adam and Eve

In a literal reading, God explains His punishments to Adam and Eve. Adam and Eve will both have sorrow. Eve will conceive, her desire will be to her husband, and her husband will rule over her. Adam will work the ground to bring forth bread.

The figurative reading provides additional insight into husband/wife relationships beyond that provided by the symbol of the rib. To begin with, President Spencer W. Kimball says that it would be good to understand the word *rule* as meaning "preside."[22] This suggests that the role of the husband and father is to lead and teach his family in the paths of truth. As the father of the home obeys Father in Heaven in righteousness, so can his wife and children then trust him and abide by the counsel that he receives through the Holy Ghost. The Doctrine and Covenants further suggests that this counsel should be given not by dictatorial means but by kindness, pure knowledge, and persuasion (see D&C 121:41–42).

Second, President Ezra Taft Benson used this part of the book of Moses as a metaphor to explain the different roles God has established for husbands and wives. He explained that

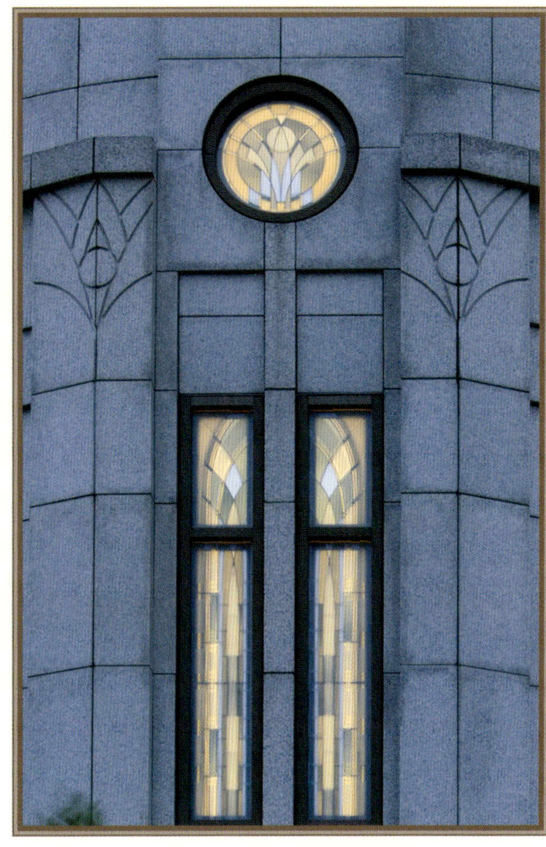

there are cases in which mothers have to leave the home and children for gainful employment. But where it is possible, the ideal is that fathers should provide physically for the family and mothers should nurture the children at home. This does not mean that each family responsibility or chore must be assigned to either one spouse or the other and that neither person should help with the other's responsibilities. It does mean, as President Benson declared in this same sermon, that "a child needs a mother more than all the things money can buy"[23] and that having the mother in the home provides a child with a sense of security different from the type of security the father can offer.

The First Presidency's *The Family: A Proclamation to the World* summarizes these teachings in this way: "By divine design, fathers are to preside over their families in love and righteousness and are responsible to provide the necessities of life and protection for their families. Mothers are primarily responsible for the nurture of their children."[24]

Doctrinally, we have already seen that when a husband and wife enter the covenant of eternal marriage, they should give up part of their individual needs to become one and devote themselves to the exaltation of their family (see Moses 3:24). The explanation of the idea of different roles in this part of the story-presentation (see Moses 4:22–25) reinforces and illuminates this principle.

The Coats of Skin

In the account, God makes Adam and Eve coats of skin to clothe them, keep them modest, and especially provide them with physical protection in mortality. For Latter-day Saints these coats call to mind the temple garment, which contributes to their modesty but more importantly stands as a symbol of their temple covenants. Latter-day Saints believe that by keeping their covenants, they are protected from sin and disobedience. In a symbolic sense, temple garments are a spiritual protection, and they remind us of the covenants we have made with God and of His promise of eternal life.

The Cherubim

After expelling Adam and Eve from the Garden of Eden, God commands that cherubim be placed at the entrance to the Garden of Eden to guard the way to the tree of life, symbolically blocking Adam and Eve from returning to God's presence. This does not suggest that the tree of life is eternally off limits. Rather, it signifies that all human beings, represented by Adam and Eve, can pass by the cherubim and enter into exaltation if they pass the test of mortality "through the Atonement of Christ . . . by obedience to the laws and ordinances of the Gospel" (Articles of Faith 1:3). The cherubim guarding the tree are symbolic reminders that the judgment

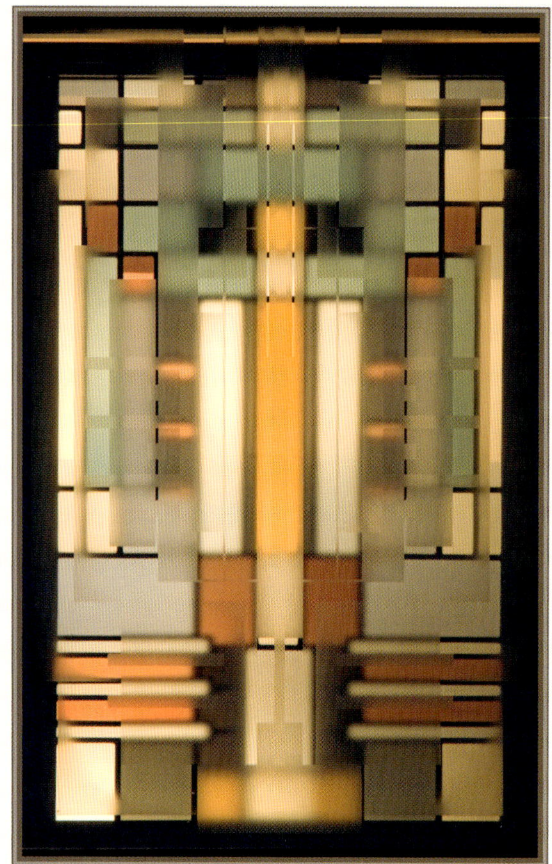

will determine whether individuals used their agency wisely, chose to make the Atonement effective in their lives, and kept their covenants.

Summary of the Fall

In summary, the account of the Fall gives great symbolic instruction on the nature of the mortal test and how it fits into God's plan. The symbol of the rib suggests that God wants husbands and wives to be eternally united and exalted in His kingdom. The trees and the fruit show that exaltation is a choice and that humans have agency to determine whether they will succeed on the journey to exaltation. The serpent symbolizes the challenges on the journey to exaltation, and it explains the nature of some of Satan's temptations. The apron encourages fallen mortals to be humble and repentant and reminds them that they need the Atonement. The curse of the serpent poetically introduces the hope of a Savior and the promise of redemption for sins committed. The instructions to Adam and Eve show how men and women can help each other in their joint goal to achieve exaltation. The coats of skin give assurance that God will help His repentant children. The cherubim represent the idea that only through the Atonement and faithful keeping of covenants can God's children return to His presence and be exalted.

Lehi's Use of the Fall in His Sermon

Together these many symbols testify that God's plan has the power to exalt His children.

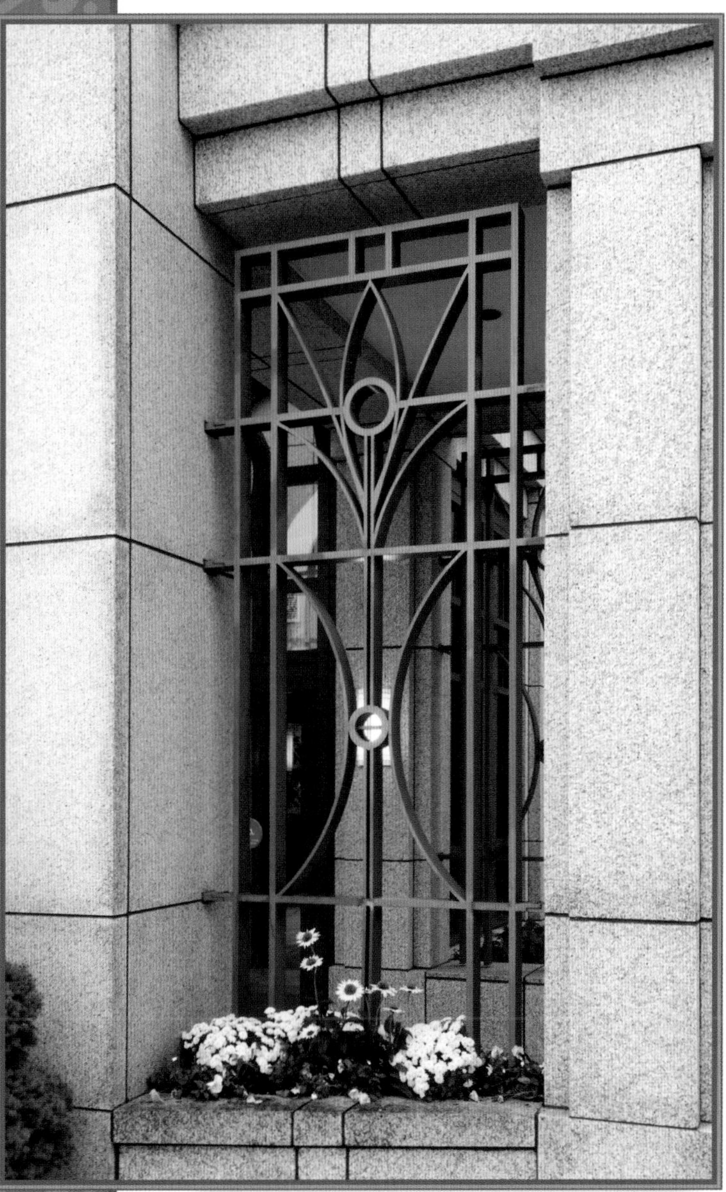

But they also show that the plan can only be activated for each individual through his or her own choices. It is for this reason that the story of the Fall is so effective in Lehi's efforts to encourage his sons to choose eternal life. His use of the doctrine of the Fall dramatically increases the power of his admonition. He tells his sons that he has read about the premortal rebellion of Satan and how the devil seeks "the misery of all mankind." He calls Satan "that old serpent" (2 Nephi 2:17–18), obviously interpreting the serpent as a symbol of Satan's deceptive tactics. He shows that mortality is a time of testing, a state of probation as he calls it (see 2 Nephi 2:21), a time when the children of men must repent.

Lehi also testifies that if Adam and Eve had not fallen, the probationary test of mortality would not be possible, because they could do no good without the possibility of sin. They could not know joy because they would not know misery. They would also have had no children, and thus God's plan to exalt His children would have been defeated because it would never have been put into effect (see 2 Nephi 2:22–23). But, Lehi explains, the plan *was* put into effect; Adam and Eve *did* fall according to the wisdom of God so that men and women could come to earth, live well, and ultimately have joy in the kingdom of God (see 2 Nephi 2:24–25). Furthermore, God would send the Messiah to redeem humanity from the negative effects of the Fall. Because there was a way provided to escape from sin, men and women are free to choose eternal life. If they do not choose this path, however, then essentially they choose captivity and death (see 2 Nephi 2:26–27). Lehi's powerful explanation of this one great choice in life—something we have seen before in the tree of life visions of both Lehi and Nephi—summarizes the pleading of an old father that his sons repent and choose exaltation.

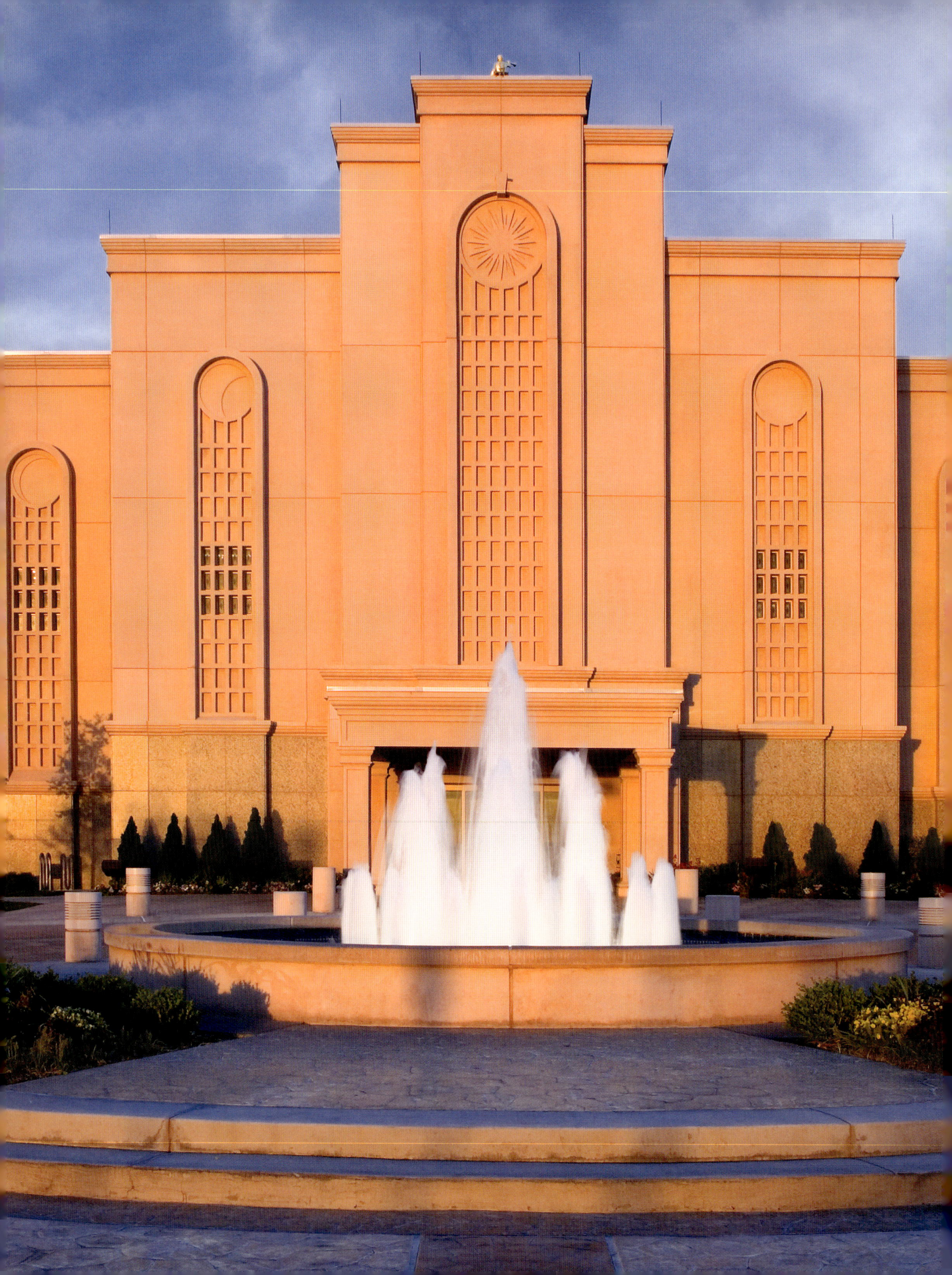

Covenants and Ascension to God

2 Nephi 31–32

Why does God require His children to receive ordinances? The common answer, "so they can show obedience," contains some truth, but it stops far short of revealing more significant insights. If taken to its logical conclusion, obedience as the only reason for ordinances characterizes God as an all-powerful being who requires submission solely for His pleasure. Nephi's last recorded sermon, centered on what he calls "the doctrine of Christ," gives a much better reason for ordinances than just the whim of God: the ordinances administer the keys of knowledge necessary to open the doors to eternal life and that they are therefore absolutely necessary for exaltation.

In fact, Nephi's teachings illustrate that even Christ had to go through the ordinance process. Nephi opens his discourse by asking why the Savior, a completely sinless individual, had to be baptized. His answer is that Christ had to witness to the Father that He would be obedient to the commandments (see 2 Nephi 31:7). In other words, Christ had to make covenants—a witness to the Father—just like the rest of God's children. As Joseph Smith said, "If a man gets a fullness of the priesthood of God, he has to get it in the same way that Jesus Christ obtained it, and that was by keeping all the commandments and obeying all the ordinances of the house of the Lord."[25] If the Son of God Himself obtained exaltation "grace by grace" (D&C 93:13) through the covenant process, then, as Nephi says, "how much more need have we, being unholy, to be baptized" (2 Nephi 31:5).

Covenants, administered in symbolic teaching ceremonies called ordinances, make individuals eligible to receive God's knowledge and the power of godliness (see D&C 84:19–20). God gives this knowledge to His children line upon line and precept by precept (see D&C 98:12) through revelation—but only after they have covenanted to use it correctly. Only when God's children have promised to discipline themselves to become disciples; only when they have promised to use God's knowledge for good and good only; only when they have agreed to consecrate themselves to the service of God and their fellow human beings will God begin to dispense the knowledge and powers of godliness. God tightly controls this process. He gives His knowledge and power a little at a time, after covenant, by revelation through the Holy Ghost to those who seek it, and He stipulates that there will be penalties—the loss of His gifts and/or membership privileges—if His children willfully use the gifts for wicked and wrong purposes. If used wisely, however, God's knowledge produces greater righteousness, which then leads to greater knowledge, which, in turn, produces greater righteousness. Thus there exists a circular relationship between an increase in personal holiness and obtaining more of God's knowledge. Elder Neal A. Maxwell explains this relationship in these terms:

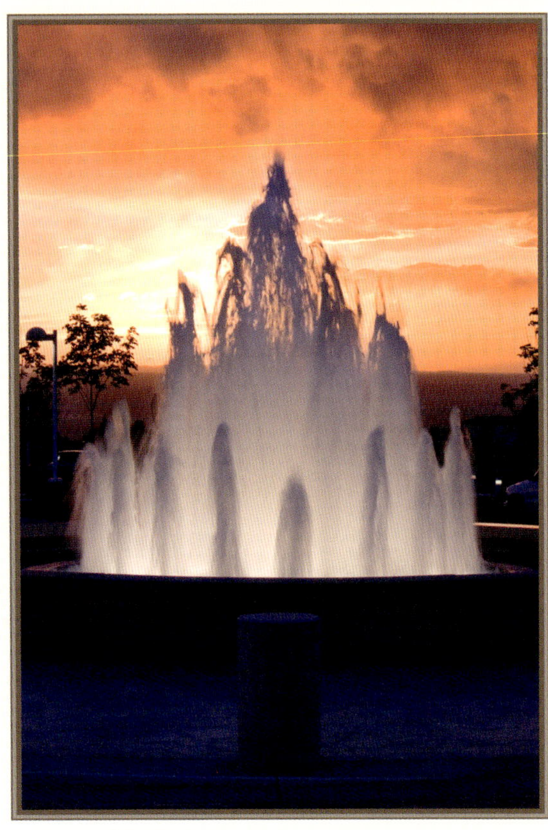

Gaining knowledge and becoming more Christlike "are two aspects of a single process" (C. Terry Warner, in *Encyclopedia of Mormonism,* 4:1490, Macmillan Co., 1992). This process is part of being "valiant" in our testimony of Jesus. Thus, while we are saved no faster than we gain a certain type of knowledge, it is also the case that we will gain knowledge no faster than we are saved! . . . So in our different understanding of knowledge and truth, behaving and knowing are inseparably linked.[26]

When Latter-day Saints keep their promises to abide by God's teachings and accept His tutoring, they allow Heavenly Father to guide them through a godhood training process that leads eventually to exaltation. Baptism initiates this process. Nephi calls it the gate to the path of eternal life and says it is the prerequisite for receiving the gift of the Holy Ghost (see 2 Nephi 31:17–18). However, Nephi also makes it very clear that the covenant of baptism is just the beginning. God expects His children, once they have access to the revelations concerning His character and will, to constantly pursue greater holiness. Nephi teaches that they must "press forward . . . in Christ . . . feasting on the word of Christ" (2 Nephi 31:20). He says that the words of Christ are given by the power of the Holy Ghost and that the Holy Ghost "will tell you all things what ye should do" (2 Nephi 32:3).

As Heavenly Father's children ascend this path to God, other gates beyond baptism occasionally appear at ascending levels. These are the temple covenants. As we take upon ourselves the more demanding and specific obligations of the higher ordinances, we become eligible for higher levels of knowledge and are expected to rise to higher levels of righteousness. By this process, and through the Atonement of Christ and the sanctifying power of the Holy Ghost, God moves His children to become like Him.

In the Old Testament, the prophet Jacob was taught this ascension/covenant-making process through his dream of a ladder. According to Elder Marion G. Romney, the principle rungs of Jacob's ladder represent the temple covenants.[27] While we may not know the full nature of these covenants between God and Jacob, scripture does reveal at least some of the details. In the Bible account, God promised Jacob land, posterity, and His accompanying influence in return for Jacob's promise that he and his posterity would bless the families of the earth (Genesis 28:13–15). According to the Bible Dictionary, these blessings are part of the Abrahamic covenant and are related to the temple blessings that are today offered in the ordinance of celestial marriage.[28] Given what we know, we can assume that the angels in Jacob's dream, who are ascending and descending on the ladder, are messengers sent from Heavenly Father to instruct Jacob concerning the covenants and prepare him for the presence of God. For that is the ultimate goal of Jacob's ascension of the ladder—at the top of the ladder God is waiting for Jacob to return to His presence.

As illustrated by Jacob's dream, as we make and keep our covenants with God, the Holy Ghost will lead us to loftier and loftier heights of truth and righteousness until at a certain point the revelations will come from God Himself. Eventually, either in this life or the next, the faithful will be raised into the presence of Jesus Christ and Heavenly Father to be taught by Them personally. On this issue Joseph Smith explained,

> After a person has faith in Christ, repents of his sins, and is baptized for the remission of his sins and receives the Holy Ghost, (by the laying on of hands), which is the first Comforter, then let him continue to humble himself before God, hungering and thirsting after righteousness, and living by every word of God, and the Lord will soon say unto him, Son, thou shalt be exalted.
>
> When the Lord has thoroughly proved him, and finds that the man is determined to serve Him at all hazards, then the man will find his calling and his election made sure, then it will be his privilege to receive the other comforter. . . .
>
> Now what is this other Comforter? It is no more nor less than the Lord Jesus Christ Himself; and this is the sum and substance of the whole matter; that when any man obtains this last Comforter, he will have the personage of Jesus Christ to attend him, or appear unto him from time to time, and even He will manifest the Father unto him, and they will take up their abode with him, and the visions of the heavens will be opened unto him, and the Lord will teach

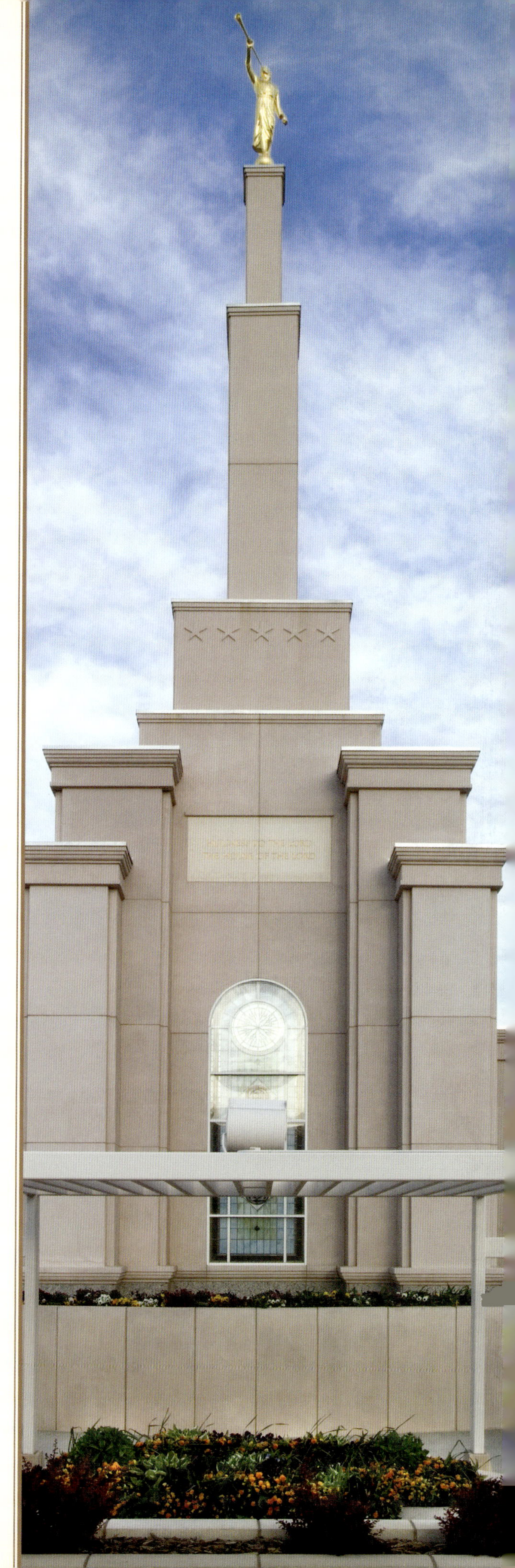

Albuquerque New Mexico Temple

Covenants and Ascension to God

The theme of the Albuquerque New Mexico temple is ascension to God. On the western side there is an obvious movement upward toward the heavens. This is emphasized by both the steplike, upward movement of the roofline and the moons and sun at the top of the stylized ladders on the façade with circles at the top.

The ascension motif is also prominent on the eastern side, where great rectangular supports rise again in a steplike manner to support the central tower that points to heaven. The moon and sun again, with the addition of stars, draw our eyes upward, as do the stylized ladders, also reminding us of the ascension to God that we can make as we receive and keep covenants and become eligible to grow in the knowledge and perfections of God. Inside the temple, patrons typically ascend a series of stairs as they progress toward the celestial room.

Scriptural examples of the ascension motif include Moses' climb to Mt. Sinai (see Exodus 3:1–6), Israel's exodus from bondage to the promised land (see Exodus 13:17–19:1; Numbers 10:10–36:13; Deuteronomy 34; Joshua 1–11), Ezekiel's heavenly council experience (see Ezekiel 1–3), the Mount of Transfiguration (see Matthew 17:1–7), John the Revelator's heavenly council experience (see Revelation 4–5), Joseph Smith's First Vision (see Joseph Smith—History 1:16–20), and Joseph Smith's vision of the three degrees of glory (see D&C 76).

Ascension to God is a theme that appears often in the Church. For instance, at baptism, members descend into the water, symbolically burying their own selfish desires, witnessing that they have given up their will to God. The ascension out of the water symbolizes new life in Christ and begins the new journey upward to God. The Apostle Paul emphasized this symbol in these terms: "Know ye not, that as many of us as were baptized into Jesus Christ were baptized into his death? Therefore we are buried with him by baptism into death: that like as Christ was raised up from the dead by the glory of the Father, even so we also should walk in newness of life" (Romans 6:3–4). Changing out of street clothes into the white baptismal clothes also represents this newness of person.

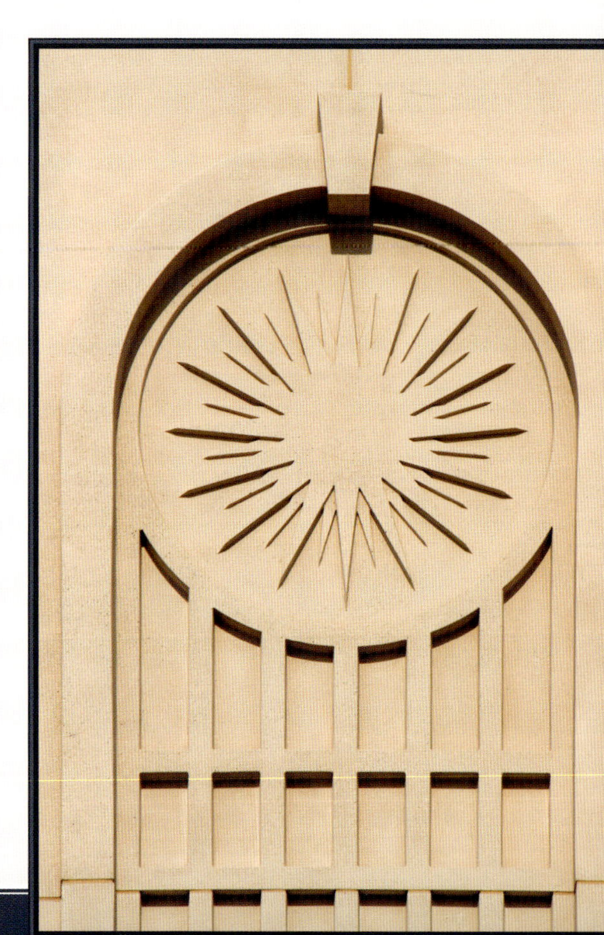

Baptism is not the only time a Latter-day Saint will encounter the theme of ascension. In fact, it appears and reappears regularly in architecture, doctrine, scripture, and ordinances. Obviously, Christ's literal descent into the despair of Gethsemane and then death on the cross, followed by His resurrection and ascent to the Father, shines as the preeminent symbol of ascension and represents our own occasional suffering in mortality, our eventual death, and our own certain, future immortality. Through Christ all shall physically rise again.

Similarly, the two main, fundamental parts of the plan of exaltation—the Fall and Atonement—also act as an instructive metaphor for humanity's possible journey upward from a selfish and willful, fallen state to the sanctified and godly character achieved by all those who have chosen redemption through Christ.

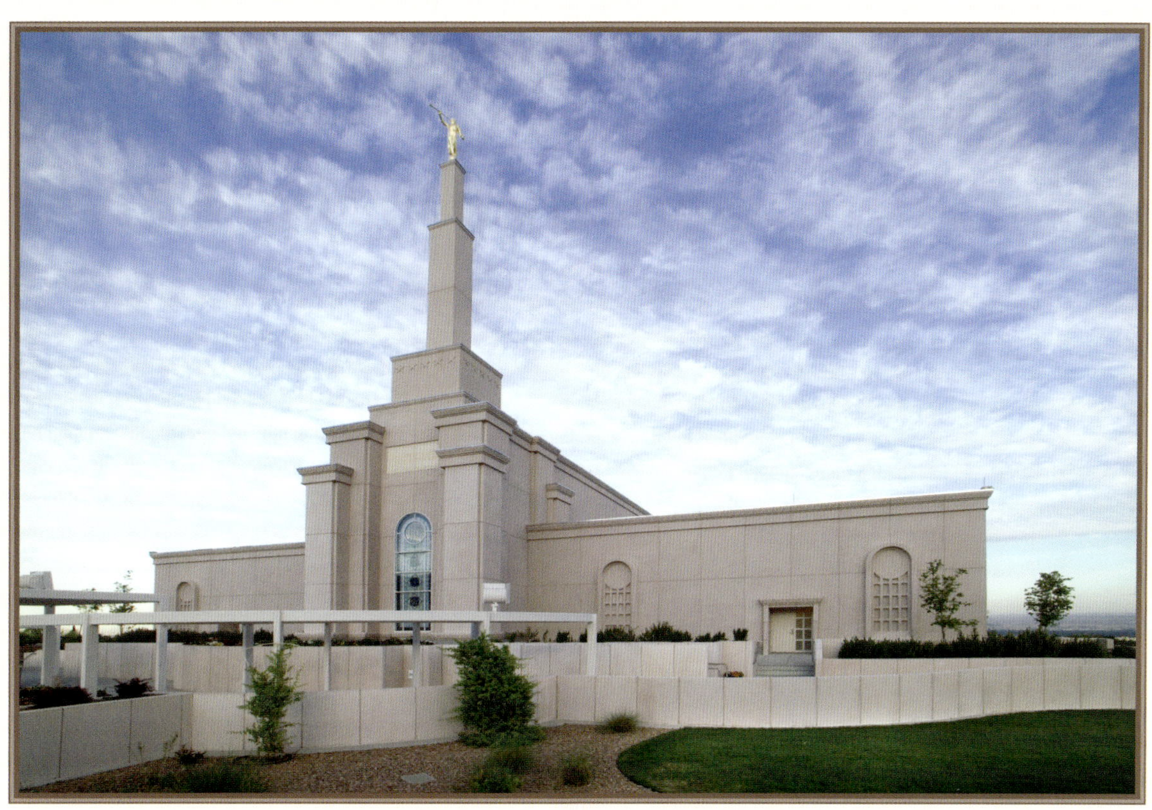

> him face to face, and he may have a perfect knowledge of the mysteries of the Kingdom of God.[29]

Nephi teaches this same spectacular principle and provides a witness that this ultimate learning experience is possible, but he also offers cautions concerning its pursuit. Having declared that the doctrine of Christ is to repent and be baptized and then to press forward, feasting on the word of Christ as revealed by the Holy Ghost, he says, "Behold this is the doctrine of Christ, and there will be no more doctrine given until after he shall manifest himself unto you in the flesh. And when he shall manifest himself unto you in the flesh, the things which he shall say unto you shall ye observe to do" (2 Nephi 32:6). The caution is to live the doctrine that is given and let the Lord decide when we are ready for the greater revelations. Until God deems us ready, we should live according to the guidance given through the Holy Ghost and not get overly anxious to look beyond those directions. It would not be a good idea, for instance, to post a "How-to-see-God checklist" on the family refrigerator! Rather, we should focus on saying daily prayers, keeping the commandments, seeking to understand the scriptural revelations available, and allowing God His own timing on this matter.

Still, Nephi cautions against going too far in the other direction. He mourns the stiffneckedness of many who "will not search knowledge, nor understand great knowledge, when it is given to them in plainness" (2 Nephi 32:7). The path to exaltation is to know God (see John 17:3). Fear of going too far is no reason to not go far enough. Nephi ends his important sermon on the doctrine of Christ with an admonition to ponder these truths and pray always that we may perform everything in life according to God's will.

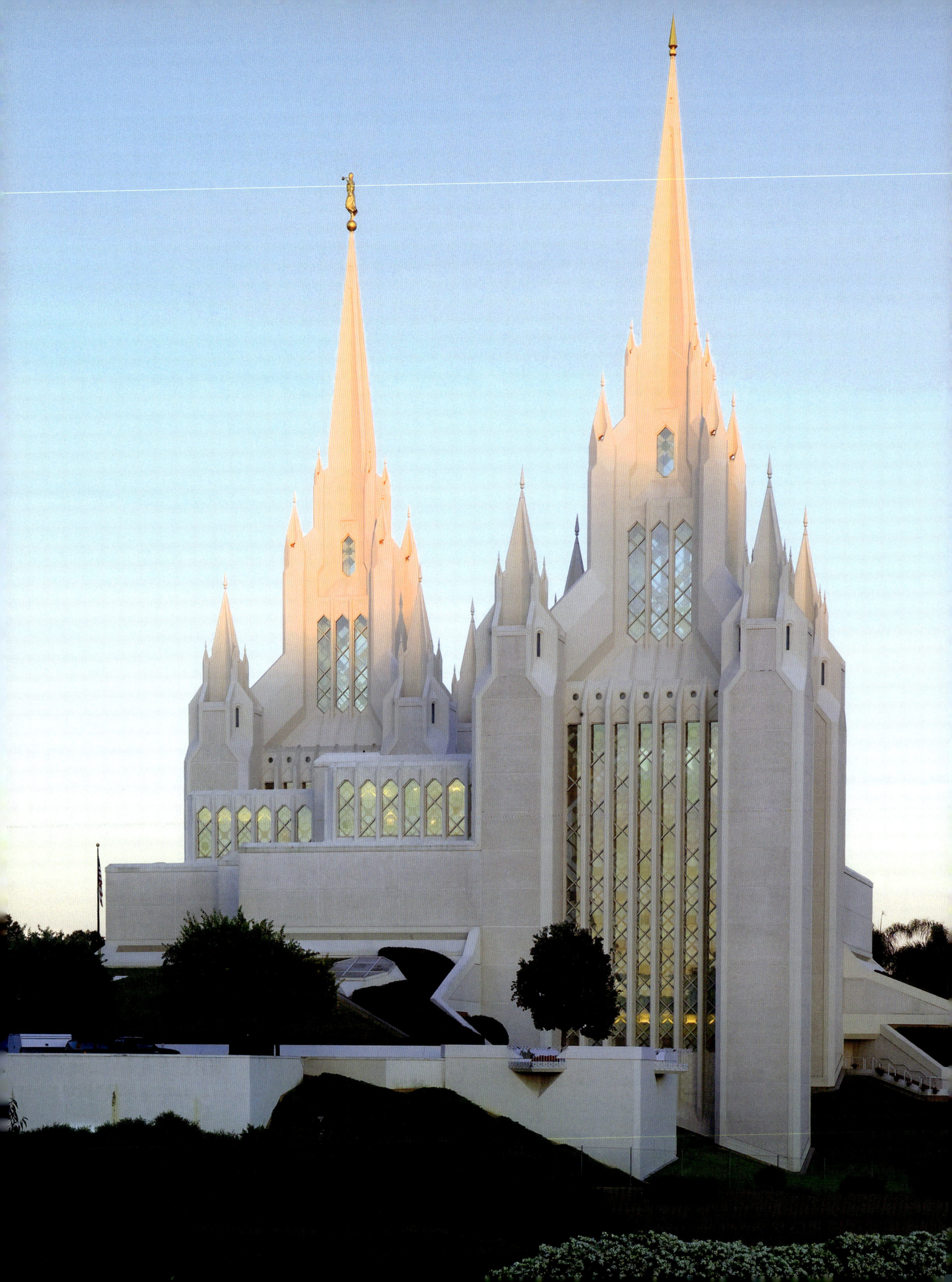

Rebirth

Mosiah 2—6

Taking upon oneself a new name is a symbol of becoming a new person. In the Old Testament, the story of Jacob exemplifies this principle. Jacob's name means "supplanter" (see Bible Dictionary, "Jacob") and typifies the struggles in his early life to gain the leadership role in his family over his slightly older brother, Esau. But after covenanting to serve God both before and during his flight to Pandan-aram (see Genesis 28:2–4, 20–21), Jacob changes directions and pursues a different journey, the journey of sanctification. Over many years and through many challenges and apparently much repentance, Jacob perseveres in the path of righteousness. In an experience that is described as wrestling[30] with God (see Genesis 32:24, 30), Jacob receives a new name, "Israel," which means "one who prevails with God" (see Bible Dictionary, "Israel"). The new name is a token that Jacob has been spiritually reborn, that his "old man is crucified with [Christ]," as Paul would say (Romans 6:6), and that he has over time become a new person. This sanctification journey, exemplified by Jacob, is the same journey of renewal described by King Benjamin in the great speech he gave at the coronation of his son Mosiah in chapters 2 through 4 of the book of Mosiah.

Those who do not want to repent should not read King Benjamin's speech. This demanding sermon pulls no punches. It teaches unequivocally that salvation can come to none except those who will repent and accept Christ as their Savior, take upon themselves His name, and become new people—be born again—through His Atonement (see Mosiah 3:17; 5:8). In a sermon built on a series of admonitions, Benjamin insists that accepting Christ's salvation means undergoing a change of heart and character, and he proclaims that exaltation requires deep humility, strict obedience to God, sacrifice, consecration, and a continual search for purity through the gospel.

Benjamin's first admonition, in Mosiah 2, is a request for his subjects to open their hearts and hear the mysteries of God (see Mosiah 2:9)—those things that are sacred and can only be understood by the Holy Spirit. Since the term *mysteries* anciently referred to sacred rites and ceremonies, it is appropriate that the rest of Benjamin's sermon follows a templelike pattern, starting with a consideration of fallen and natural man and then constantly moving upward by degrees through the obligations necessary for holiness and eternal life. Furthermore, Benjamin's speech ends with his people making a covenant of obedience to God, a key component of any temple experience.

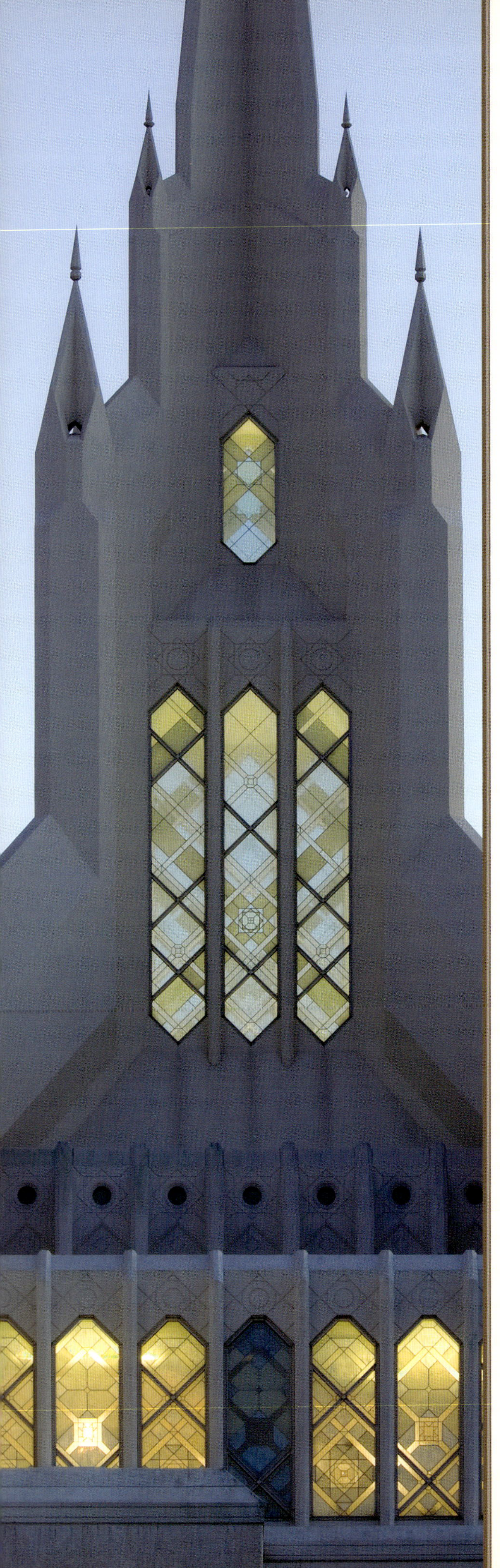

Benjamin's admonitions on fallen man, in chapter two, run contrary to all of the accepted "modern wisdom" concerning the promotion of people's self-esteem. Instead of telling his subjects how good they are and how proud he is of them, he declares that he and they are not even equal to the dust of the earth (see Mosiah 2:25–26) and that they would have to consider themselves unprofitable servants even if they served God with their whole souls (see Mosiah 2:21). His words are not meant to demean anyone. Rather, Benjamin knows that if his people want to be saved they will need the intense humility that his words are intended to provoke. Salvation requires, according to Benjamin, that individuals serve each other throughout their lives.

King Benjamin uses his own example to illustrate the type of service his people should render—service that promotes a fair and equitable society. He declares that he has used his office not for promotion of himself or his family but for service to his people, that he has not sought riches or servitude from the Nephites, and that he has not exacted heavy taxes but has used his authority to see that his people did not commit injustice (see Mosiah 2:12–14). He does not negate the value of other noble types of service, such as caring for the elderly and sick; visiting the afflicted; raising righteous families; and donating time to churches, charities, and other good causes. In fact, he applauds them and promotes them. Still, overarching his comments on service is the idea that he has used his high position not for self-promotion but to ensure the well-being of all the people. King Benjamin's example and words promote a conscious effort to help create an equitable Zionlike society. And it is because it takes deep humility for those who have a bigger piece of the pie to redivide the pie with those who have less that Benjamin so strongly challenges his people to be humble. It is this type of deep humility and concern for others, this type of law-of-consecration approach, that Benjamin especially promotes as the practice that will lead to salvation.

Benjamin's next set of admonitions, in chapter three, introduces the "born again" metaphor, employing the phrase "children of men" several times as a designation for fallen people who need such a rebirth to become the "children of God." He announces, for instance, that an angel has told him that the Lord Omnipotent will come to earth to take upon Himself a physical body and dwell among the children of men (see Mosiah 3:5). Continuing in the same vein, he declares that Christ will come and cast out the "evil spirits which dwell in the hearts of the children of men" (Mosiah 3:6); that He will come so "that salvation might come unto the children of men even through faith on his name" (Mosiah 3:9); that His coming and resurrection will bring a righteous judgment to the children of men (see Mosiah 3:10); and, finally, that there is "no other name given nor any other way nor means whereby salvation can come unto the children of men, only in and through the name of Christ, the Lord Omnipotent" (Mosiah 3:17). The assessment is clear: the *children of men* must become the *children of Christ* to receive salvation. They must become children again—"submissive, meek, humble, patient, full of love," and "willing to submit" to God as a child submits to his father (Mosiah 3:19).

Benjamin's final series of admonitions, in chapter four, insightfully illuminates the reason for this high level of meekness and submission: spiritual rebirth cannot be achieved without God's help. A holy life is too daunting for the natural man alone. Only by submitting to God's guidance can we receive the necessary direction and sanctifying power that enables a "child of man" to become a "child of Christ."

Benjamin's catalog of the conditions of exaltation (see Mosiah 4:8–30)—ordered in an ever-ascending demand for holiness—starts with an exhortation to admit our deep need for God's mercy and ends with a challenge to be altogether righteous in both body and spirit. Beginning simply, King Benjamin tells his people that all those who desire salvation must believe in God and believe that God has all wisdom and power. He tells them that they must repent and ask God for forgiveness. He then states that seekers of salvation must remember their own nothingness before God and call on Heavenly Father daily in order to retain a remission of sins and to grow in the knowledge of God and, presumably, in order to obtain the power necessary to be like Christ. Benjamin's admonitions then include the charge to not injure each other;

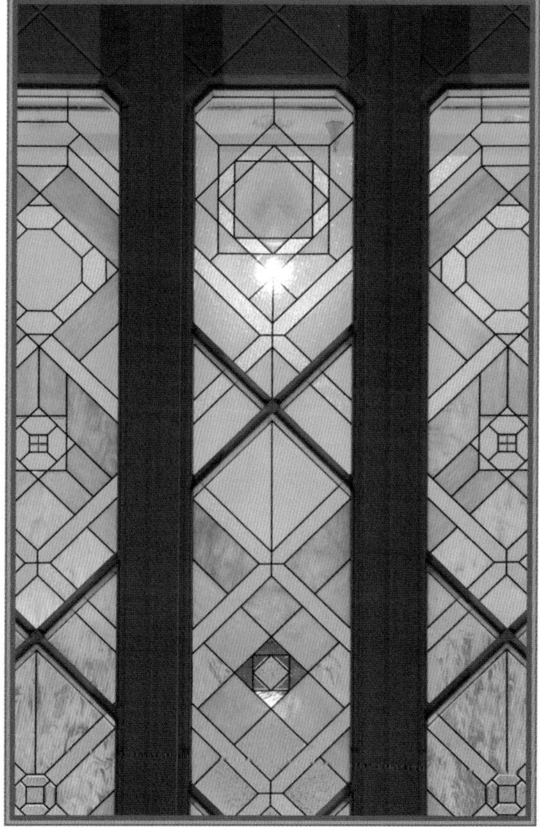

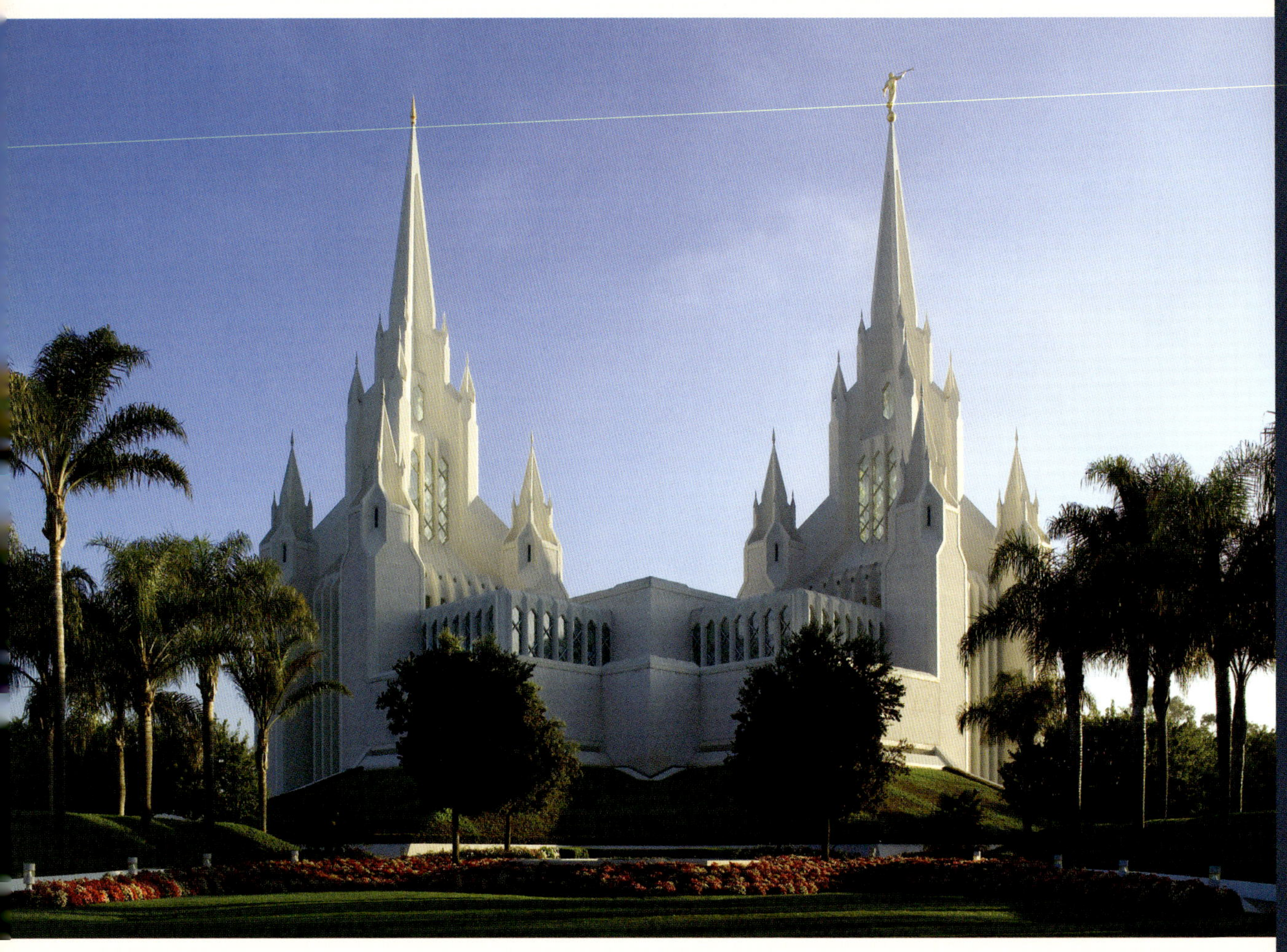

to give every human being his or her due; to materially support our families and teach them the laws of God; and to not allow our children to quarrel and follow the devil, but to teach them the truth and to love one another.

Expanding the scope of an individual's influence, King Benjamin next teaches that the children of Christ will also succor those in need—not judging beggars but giving to them, in order and with wisdom. There is much of the law of the gospel in these admonitions, as well as obedience, sacrifice, and the law of consecration. Benjamin's final admonition—to mind one's thoughts, words, and deeds—sounds somewhat like the Savior's admonition to become perfect as He and His Father are (see 3 Nephi 12:48). Such a rebirth, to become as God is, requires deep individual humility plus God's grace and the sanctifying power of the Atonement.

The power of King Benjamin's words changed his listeners' hearts. By choice, they truly became new creatures, children of Christ who had "no more disposition to do evil, but to do good continually" (Mosiah 5:2). Their desires changed. What they experienced was similar to what President Lorenzo Snow described as happening to early Saints in this dispensation:

> When the Latter-day Saints received the Gospel in the nations afar, and when the voice of the Almighty to them was, to leave the lands of their fathers, to leave their kindred as

San Diego California Temple

Rebirth

The striking light and pronounced verticality inspire all who see the San Diego California Temple, but it is the many repeating patterns involving the octagon and the number eight that make this sacred structure symbolically powerful. According to Bill Lewis, the architect, there are more than 10,000 eight-sided figures on the San Diego Temple.[31] In fact, the octagon motif is so widespread that even the pavement in the street on the temple's east side contains this symbolically remarkable figure.

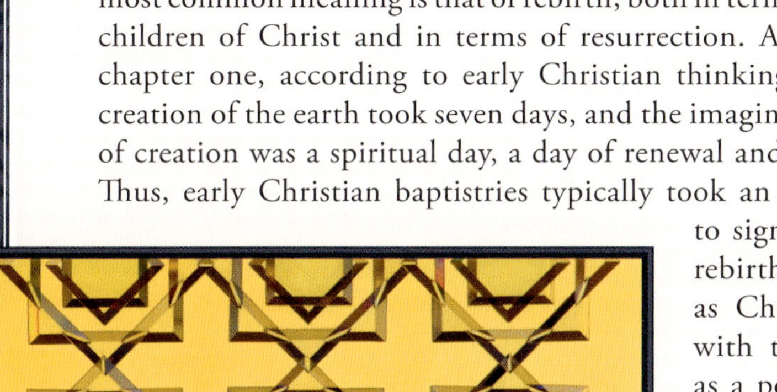

Traditionally, an eight-sided figure on a Christian building carries two meanings with great significance for Latter-day Saints. The most common meaning is that of rebirth, both in terms of becoming children of Christ and in terms of resurrection. As discussed in chapter one, according to early Christian thinking the physical creation of the earth took seven days, and the imaginary eighth day of creation was a spiritual day, a day of renewal and starting over. Thus, early Christian baptistries typically took an octagon form to signify individual rebirth as well as Christ's Resurrection. Similarly, the San Diego Temple, with thousands of octagons as its dominant motif, stands as a powerful monument to rebirth through Christ and as a testimony to the Resurrection.

The second significant meaning of an eight-sided figure is as the seal of Melchizedek. The most interesting historical use of these overlapping square outlines, intersecting at a right angle, is found in a mosaic in St. Apollinare in Classe, a sixth-century Italian church. This mosaic shows the seal of Melchizedek[32] positioned on an altar with Abel on the left, Melchizedek behind, and Abraham and Isaac to the right—four Old Testament figures whose sacrifices foreshadow Christ's atoning sacrifice. The hand of God the Father emerges from the curtain to the left to signal His presence and His acceptance of the sacrifices offered.

For Latter-day Saints, the seal of Melchizedek should remind us that it is the Melchizedek Priesthood that administers the ordinances of exaltation in our modern temples and thereby manifests the power of godliness (see D&C 84:19–21). It is here, in these holy places, that Latter-day Saints receive the promise of the ultimate rebirth—sanctification and the potential to become like God.

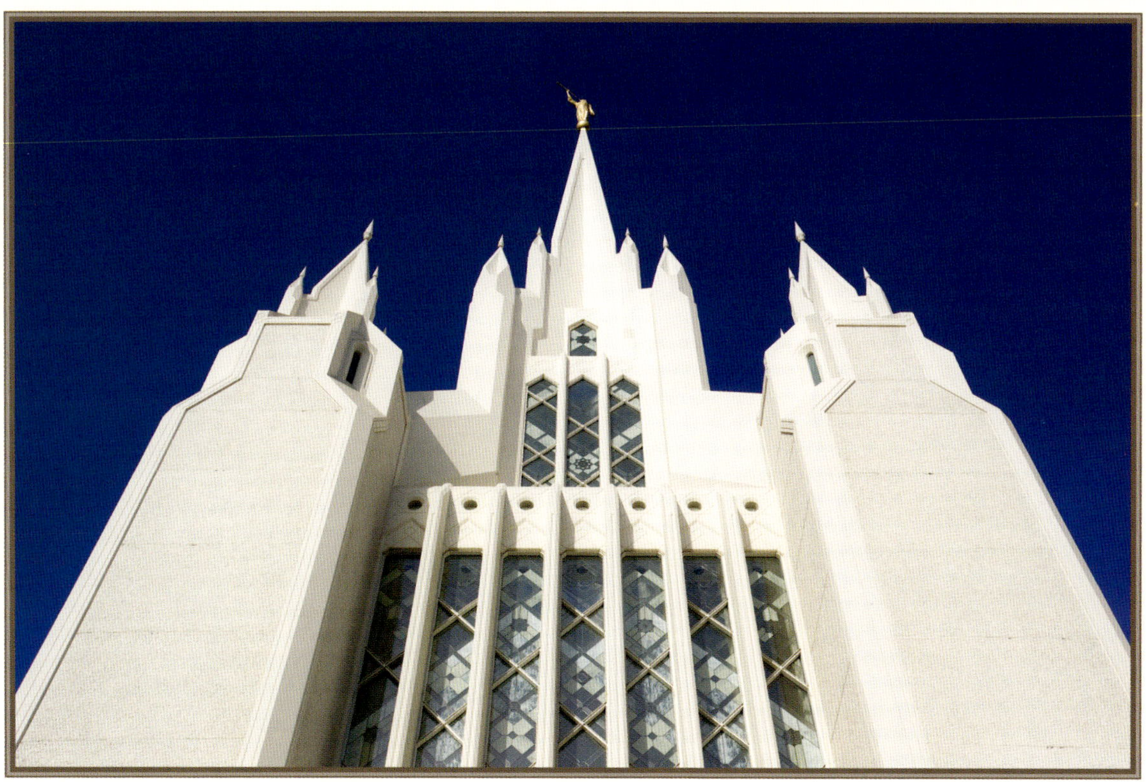

> Abraham did, so far as they complied with this requirement, so far as they were walking in obedience to this law; and they were as perfect as men could be under the circumstances, and in the sphere in which they were acting, not that they were perfect in knowledge or power, etc.; but in their feelings, in their integrity, motives and determination. . . . Therefore, we must seek the ability to keep this law, to sanctify our motives, desires, feelings and affections, that they may be pure and holy, and our will in all things be subservient to the will of God, and have no will of our own except to do the will of our Father. Such a man in his sphere is perfect, and commands the blessing of God in all that he does and wherever he goes.[33]

As President Lorenzo Snow suggests, the desire to submit to God's will is the means of becoming perfect, as far as that is possible in this life. As he explains, it is not possible to become perfect in this life in knowledge or power, but perfection of motives, desires, and feelings is something that we can and should seek after. It was this state of rebirth in desire and submission to God that caused the Nephites listening to King Benjamin to accept a covenant of obedience (see Mosiah 5:5).

After they make this covenant, King Benjamin's people receive a new name, the name of Christ, as a symbol of their rebirth. They become, so to speak, Christ's sons and daughters. This is, of course, figurative and not literally true—Christ did not beget them physically. Rather, the new name is a powerful spiritual symbol that Benjamin's people are determined to become like Christ. They are no longer "children of men" but have assumed the motives, desires, and feelings of Christ. They have begun the ascension to become as God is. As Elder Dallin H. Oaks states, "Those who are qualified by faith and

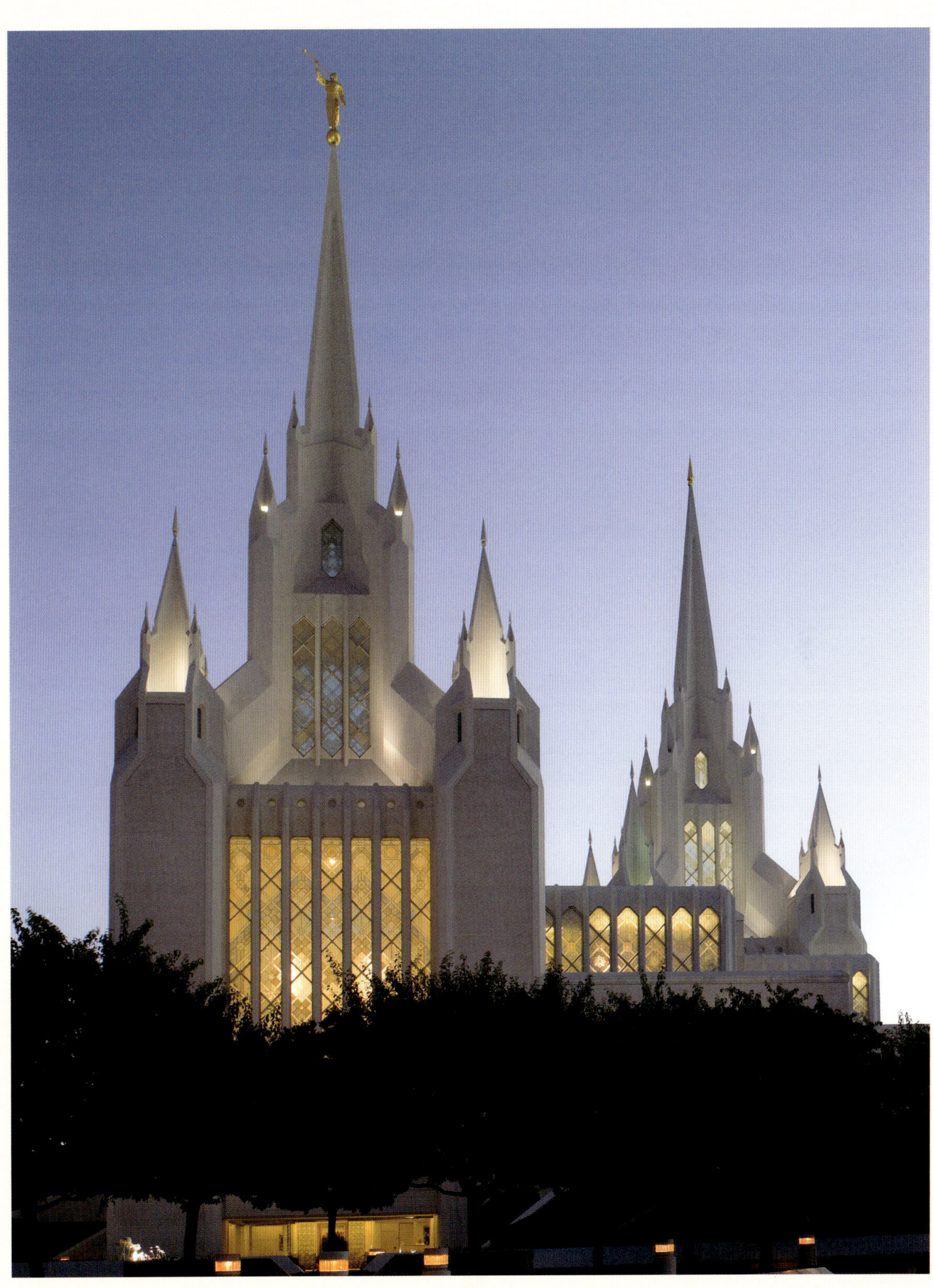

repentance and compliance with the laws and ordinances of the gospel will have their sins borne by the Lord Jesus Christ. In spiritual and figurative terms they will become the sons and daughters of Christ, heirs to his kingdom. These are they who will be called by his name in the last day."[34]

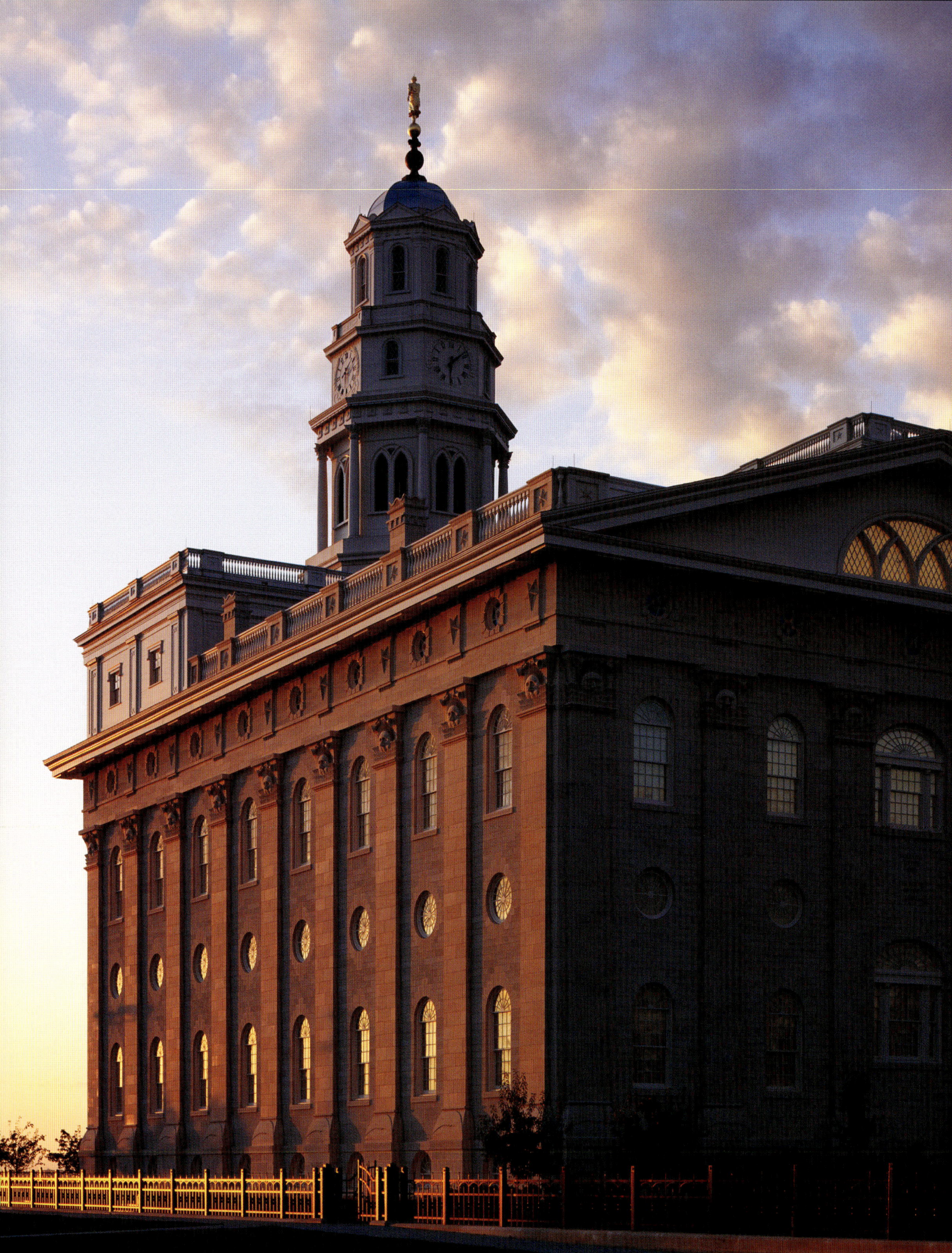

Eternal Perspectives

Alma 39—42

Temple endowments create eternal perspective. They give insight to the meaning of life and help us understand the reasons why we should endure righteously during the struggles and difficulties of mortality. They empower us to travel the journey of life with answers to life's great questions, much as the endowment-like experience that Moses had on Mount Sinai empowered him to succeed in his journey to deliver Israel from Egypt.

As part of his instruction on the mount, Moses saw a vision of this world and of space (see Moses 1:8, 27–29). God's objective in showing creation stories in endowments seems to be, at the very least, to encourage His children to ask questions so that they can be more easily taught. In Moses' case, the glimpse into eternity had its desired effect. He asked how and why the worlds were created (see Moses 1:30)—two great questions that showed that his heart and mind were open and ready to be taught. In response, God showed Moses that the worlds were created by the Son of God as part of the Father's plan to exalt His children. This deeper perspective of God's love and power prepared Moses for his assignment into Egypt, convincing him that God would be victorious and that God had a great reason for the mission (see Moses 1:31–32, 39).

For Latter-day Saints, the modern temple endowment prepares them for their own God-given individual assignments. The endowment does this, as we learned from Elder Widstoe in chapter one, by teaching the doctrines concerning "man's eternal journey from the dim beginning towards his possible glorious destiny."[35]

The doctrines of the gospel concerning man's eternal journey are the great "why." They provide reasons for the moral laws that God expects us to live. They give meaning and perspective to the trials of life and the requirements that Heavenly Father places upon His covenant people. Fortified with this knowledge, Latter-day Saints have significant advantage over the powers of evil in the battle for salvation. Without it, the fight to live God's commandments is far more confusing. The best scriptural example of this principle—that doctrines supply the reasons for keeping the commandments—comes from Alma's great lecture to his son Corianton, who struggled with sins of immorality. The instruction on doctrine that Alma gives is not a formal endowment, but because it so well illustrates the connection between eternal perspective and knowing doctrine, it works as an informal endowment that illustrates this crucial principle.

Understandably grieved over Corianton's sins, Alma at first moralizes some in his lecture to his son—a normal reaction for most parents. He tells Corianton that "these things are an abomination in the sight of the Lord"; that unless he repents, his crimes "will stand as a testimony against [him] at the last day"; and that his conduct greatly impeded the missionary work among the Zoramites (Alma 39:5, 8, 11). Alma clearly rebukes his son for his behavior. However, the majority of Alma's lecture is notably an explanation of doctrine, not a chastisement. Alma wisely recognizes that his son's immorality is a symptom of deep spiritual confusion on crucially important doctrines and that the real solution to the immorality is to correct the underlying disbelief and misunderstanding.

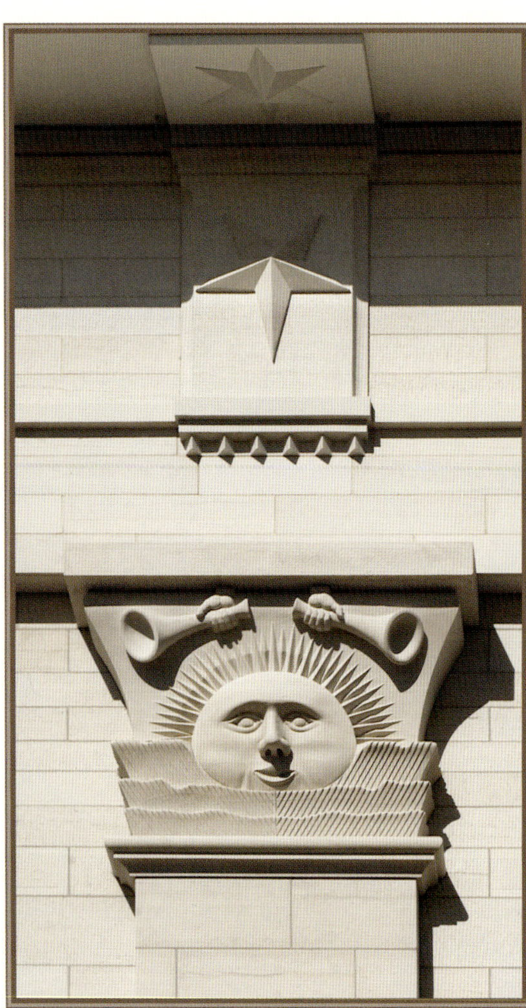

The first of Corianton's doubts concerns the prophesied coming of Christ, particularly the possibility of knowing beforehand concerning the Lord's Atonement (see Alma 39:15–17). Alma assures Corianton that God loves all His children, no matter when they are born, and that it is just as easy for God to send an angel to teach about the redemption prior to Christ's birth as it is after.

Alma next addresses Corianton's doubts about the resurrection by explaining three important points. First, he testifies that there will be a resurrection for everyone, both good and evil. He seems quite unconcerned about the timing of the resurrection, whether there is one time or several different periods, only that the resurrection is a reality for everyone (see Alma 40:4–5). Second, Alma explains the nature of the spirit world. He says that for the righteous, paradise is a state of happiness—a state of rest and peace—while for the wicked, the spirit world is a state of awful anticipation of the wrath of God (see Alma 40:12–14). This explanation of paradise as a *state* of the soul in the spirit world rather than a *place* allows Alma to emphasize the critical need for repentance. The spirit world evidently occupies space in one way or another, but where it exists is not nearly as important to Alma as is its nature. He wants Corianton to understand that "wickedness never was happiness" (Alma 41:10)—not here on earth and not in the next world. More to the point, Alma wants his son to understand that the consequences of wicked choices must be paid for and cannot be escaped by a change of location. Death will not make things better. Only repentance can do that. If we choose wickedness in this life, our natures will carry the scars of those choices because, as Amulek taught, "that same spirit which doth possess your bodies at the time that ye go out of this life, that same spirit will have power to possess your body in that eternal world" (Alma 34:34). Accentuating the pain of sin even further, Alma's third point stresses that the consequences for wickedness continue to exist even after resurrection. He states that after resurrection the righteous will "shine forth in the kingdom of God" and the wicked will "die as to things pertaining to things of righteousness . . . they drink the dregs of a bitter cup" (Alma 40:26). Alma's teachings reveal that there is no escape from unhappiness except through repentance. If our natures are wicked, without repentance we will suffer in this life and in the spirit world and even after our resurrection. A person's sinful nature will still exist after resurrection unless that person uses the atoning blood of Christ to change that nature.

The third of Corianton's doubts naturally follows Alma's teachings on the nature of the soul in the spirit world and on resurrection. Corianton is apparently not sure that the restoration of good to good and evil to evil is a true doctrine. Alma spends most of Alma 41 explaining and testifying that it is indeed true, that it is "requisite with the justice of God that men should be judged according to their works," and that if a person's works and desires are good, then good will be restored to them in the Resurrection (Alma 41:3). If a person has chosen to live a life "contrary to the nature of God, . . . they are in a state contrary to the nature of happiness" and the meaning of the word *restoration* is "to bring back again evil for evil, or carnal for carnal, or devilish for devilish—good for that which is good" (Alma 41:11, 13). Our characters, built out of our own choices, travel with us until we decide to change our characters.

Corianton's final doubt is that it does not seem right for God to punish sinners (see

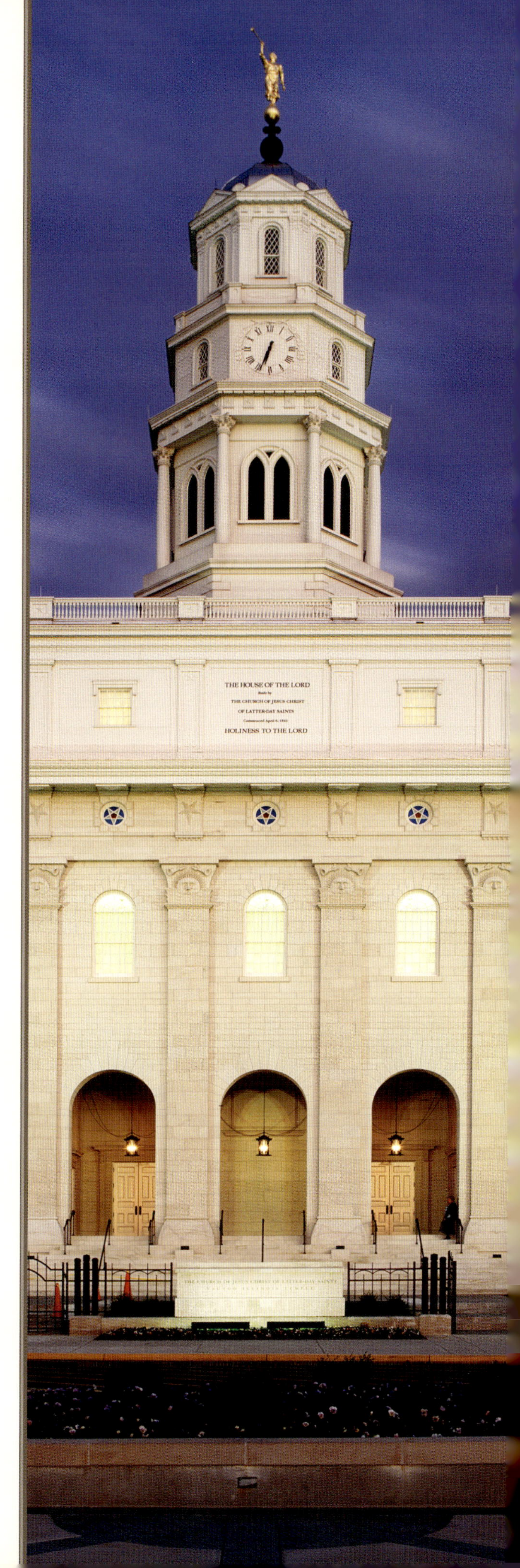

Nauvoo Illinois Temple

Eternal Perspectives

The light-centered symbols of the heavens at the Nauvoo Illinois Temple direct our attention to God and His purposes. They point us to an eternal perspective that challenges us to live better lives. They challenge us to contemplate matters of eternal significance and inspire us to reach higher and work harder in emulating the life of our true light, Jesus Christ.

Standing at the bottom of the temple, feet on the earth, looking upward, the viewer is transported heavenward, past the moon and the sun, past the stars, and into heaven beyond. This particular order of the heavenly bodies directs the mind to seek God and His kingdom. Each of these symbols works collectively—as a scale model of the universe—and individually to lead the mind to contemplate the mysteries of godliness.

This order of the heavenly bodies repeats itself again and again on each of the thirty pilasters. As Elder James E. Talmage stated, referring to the original Nauvoo Temple symbols, "each pilaster presented in hewn relief the crescent moon, and ended above in a capital of cut stone depicting the face of the sun allegorically featured, with a pair of hands holding horns. Above the capitals was a frieze or cornice in which appeared thirty star-stones."[36] This repeated order lifts our eyes heavenward, and we can see the same order recreated on the new Nauvoo Temple.

Individually, each symbol adds dimension to this heavenly contemplation. The sun bursting forth from the three cloud-veils, for instance, could represent the light and truth of God the Father ready to shine forth and be given freely to all who will receive it. The inverted star above it, pointing to the sun, is the morning and evening star, the first and last star to appear in the sky at daybreak and dawn, a symbol of Christ (see Revelation 2:28; 22:16). It is literally the planet Venus, which reflects the light of the sun, just as Christ points the way to and reflects the light of the Father.

The stained-glass windows with the inverted pointed stars surrounded by the twelve stones also represent Christ as the central focus for all of Israel, just as the tabernacle of Moses, positioned at the center of the camp of Israel, surrounded by the tents of the twelve tribes on all sides, also signified the centrality of God (see Numbers 2:1–34).

The six-pointed stars above the inverted five-pointed ones represent real stars in the heavens, as the temple symbolism continues to draw the viewer's gaze upward into heavenly spheres and beyond.

Taken as a whole, the Nauvoo Temple testifies of the Father and the Son and moves us to seek Their kingdom, encouraging us to use this eternal perspective to overcome the difficulties of mortality.

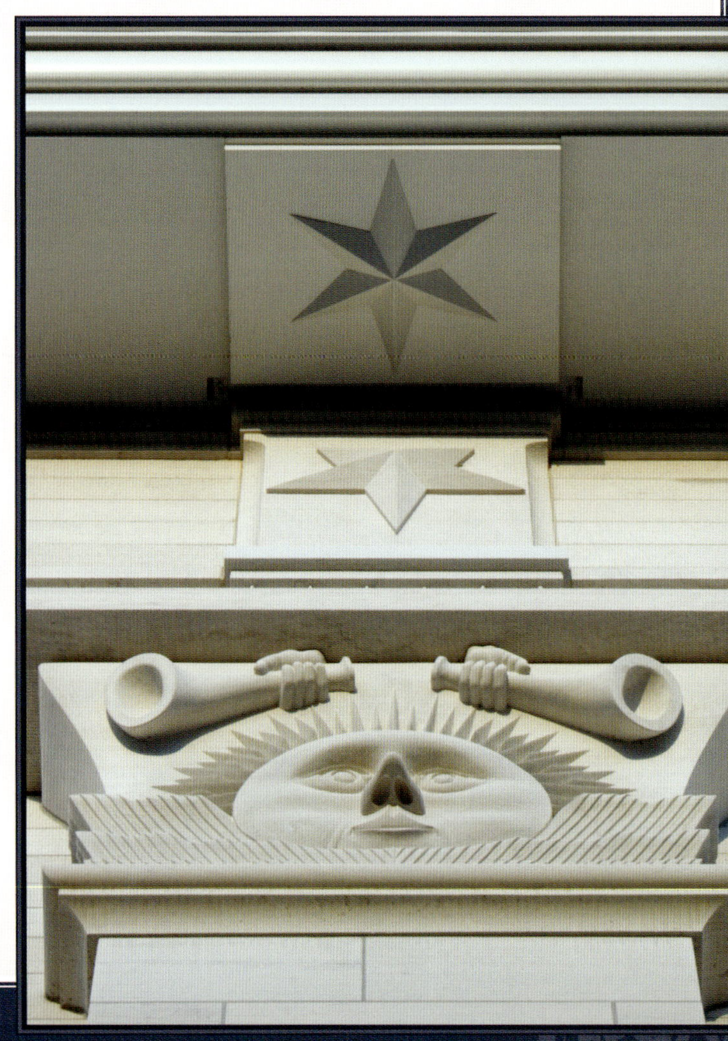

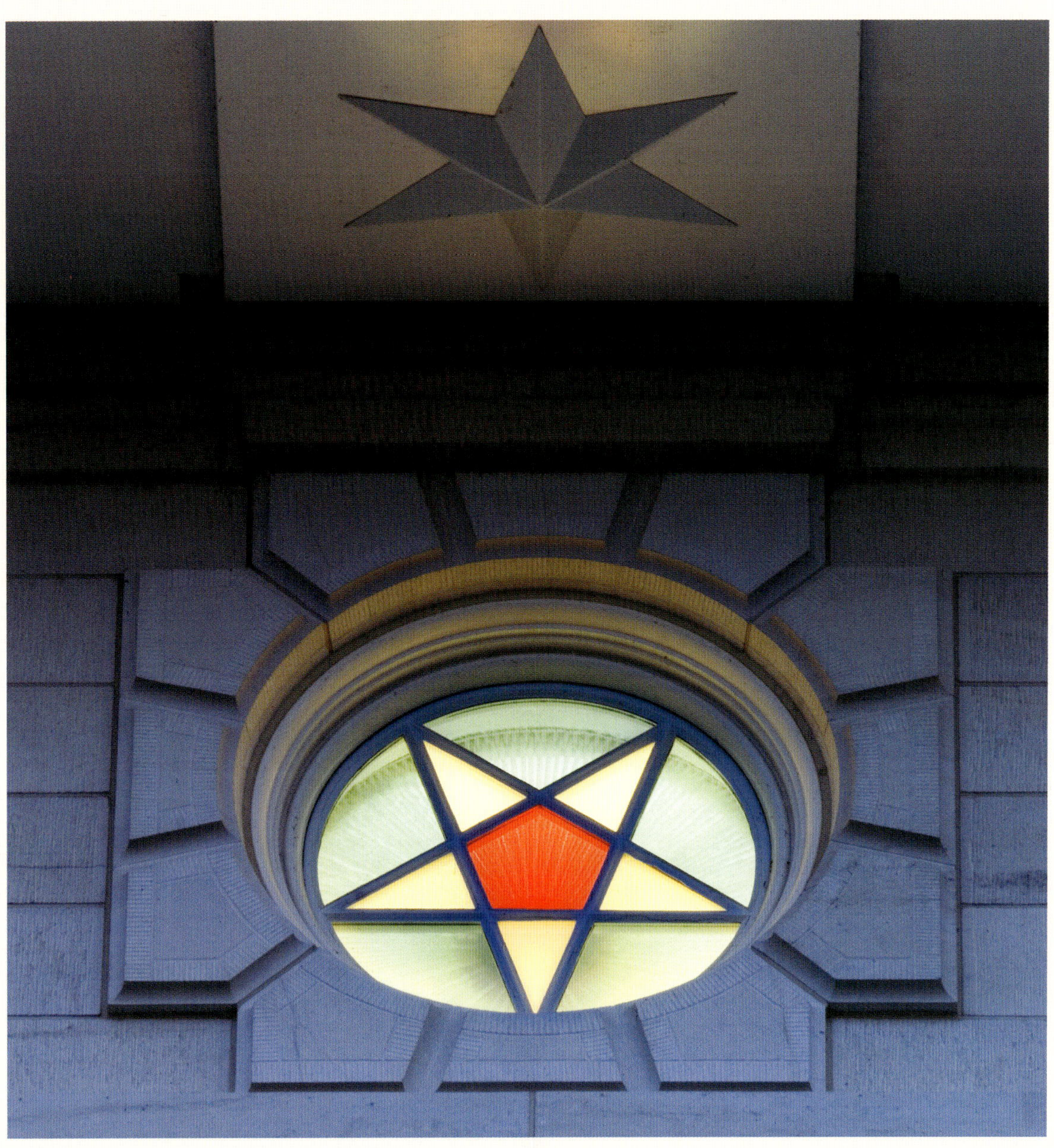

Alma 42:1). But Alma uses the doctrine of the Fall to explain that punishment is simply the natural consequence of both a person's choices and his or her refusal to use the Atonement to overcome the accompanying consequences. He shows that we are sent from the presence of God to be tested in a probationary time—mortality. This test requires that we be cut off from the presence of God so that we are free to follow our own will, and this is all set up according to the plan of happiness (see Alma 42:2, 4, 7, 9). He states that since by the Fall humankind had become carnal, sensual, and devilish, "this probationary state became a state for them to prepare" for the presence of the Lord by repentance and acceptance of the plan of redemption. God Himself atoned for the sins of the world and made possible the plan of mercy, but if we will not accept mercy by repentance, then justice must be applied to us or God would cease to be God (see Alma 42:10–15). Thus, as Alma summarizes, God brings to pass His eternal purposes

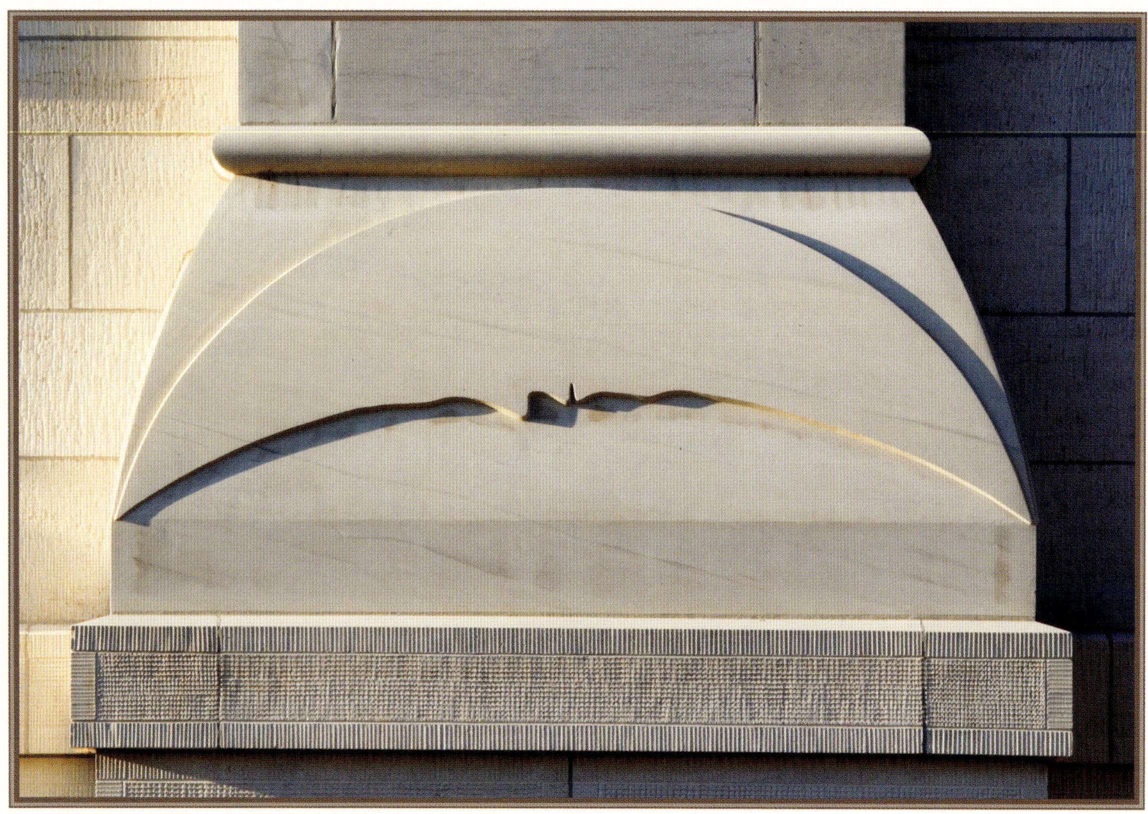

and those who want to accept salvation can, but no one will be compelled (see Alma 42:26–27). God cannot force us to change our natures and become like Him, and since a carnal nature is contrary to the nature of happiness, those who choose to remain carnal choose their own punishment.

Alma's powerful explanation of the plan of happiness had its desired effect. Endowed with new understanding of the eternal perspective behind the commandments he was being told to follow, Corianton repented. Mormon relates that he again accepted the responsibility of preaching the word of God within about a year of his father's counsel and instruction (see Alma 49:30).

The teaching of doctrine as a means of helping people gain an eternal perspective and thereby bringing them to repentance does not always work. Not everyone will choose to be saved. But as Alma states so well, speaking of his own people, "the preaching of the word had a great tendency to lead the people to do that which was just—yea, it had had more powerful effect upon the minds of the people than the sword, or anything else" (Alma 31:5). Or as Elder Boyd K. Packer has said, "True doctrine, understood, changes attitudes and behavior. The study of the doctrines of the gospel will improve behavior quicker than a study of behavior will improve behavior."[37] Teaching the doctrine works better than cajoling, moralizing, or threatening. It instructs and invites by "persuasion, by long-suffering, by gentleness and meekness, and by love unfeigned; By kindness, and pure knowledge" (D&C 121:41–42). It influences people to use their agency to leave the natural man behind and become like God. Doctrine is the "why" that best convinces men and women to adopt the "what" of gospel morality.

The temple endowment powerfully incorporates this relationship between the "why" of doctrine and the "what" of morality to give temple-goers the eternal perspective they need. It uses doctrine to remind Latter-day Saints of their potential for exaltation and then administers the covenants that can make the Atonement fully effective in their lives. In the temple, the Saints learn where they came from, the nature of mortal life, and the possibility of glory and exaltation in God's kingdom. They learn that they live in a fallen world so that they can be tested, that they will occasionally make mistakes because of the nature of the test, and that God has provided a Savior and a plan to help them overcome their mistakes and even their sins. They learn that the plan requires the grace and mercy of the Father and the Son, but that it also requires the willing acceptance of this atoning power by covenant. As we discussed in chapter five, the temple covenants, if kept, make the Atonement fully effective in the soul of a Latter-day Saint. The covenants bind us

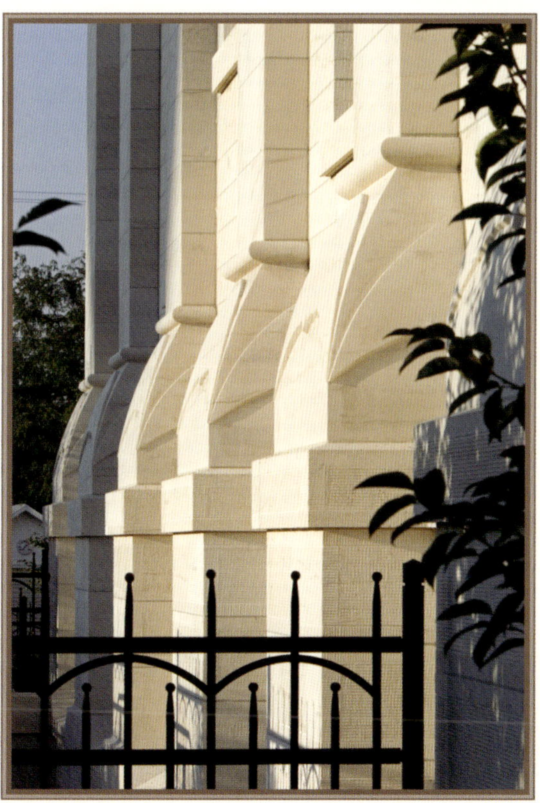

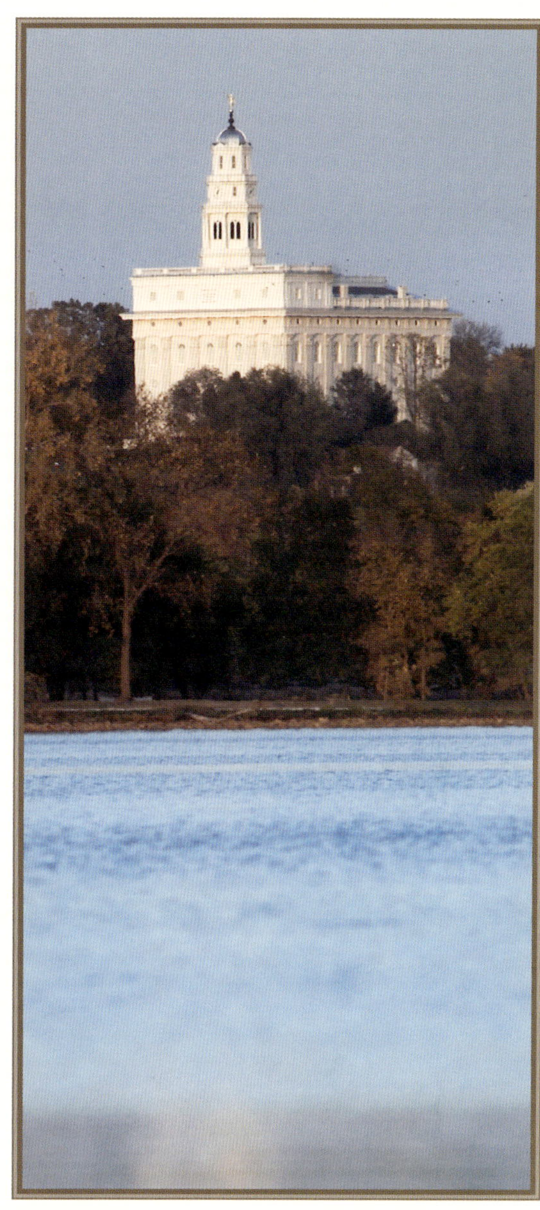

to a moral standard that makes us eligible to receive the knowledge and powers of God. The doctrines inspire us to keep the covenants and to have faith that the goal of exaltation is obtainable and that the eventual reward is worth the pain and challenges of living a disciplined and moral life.

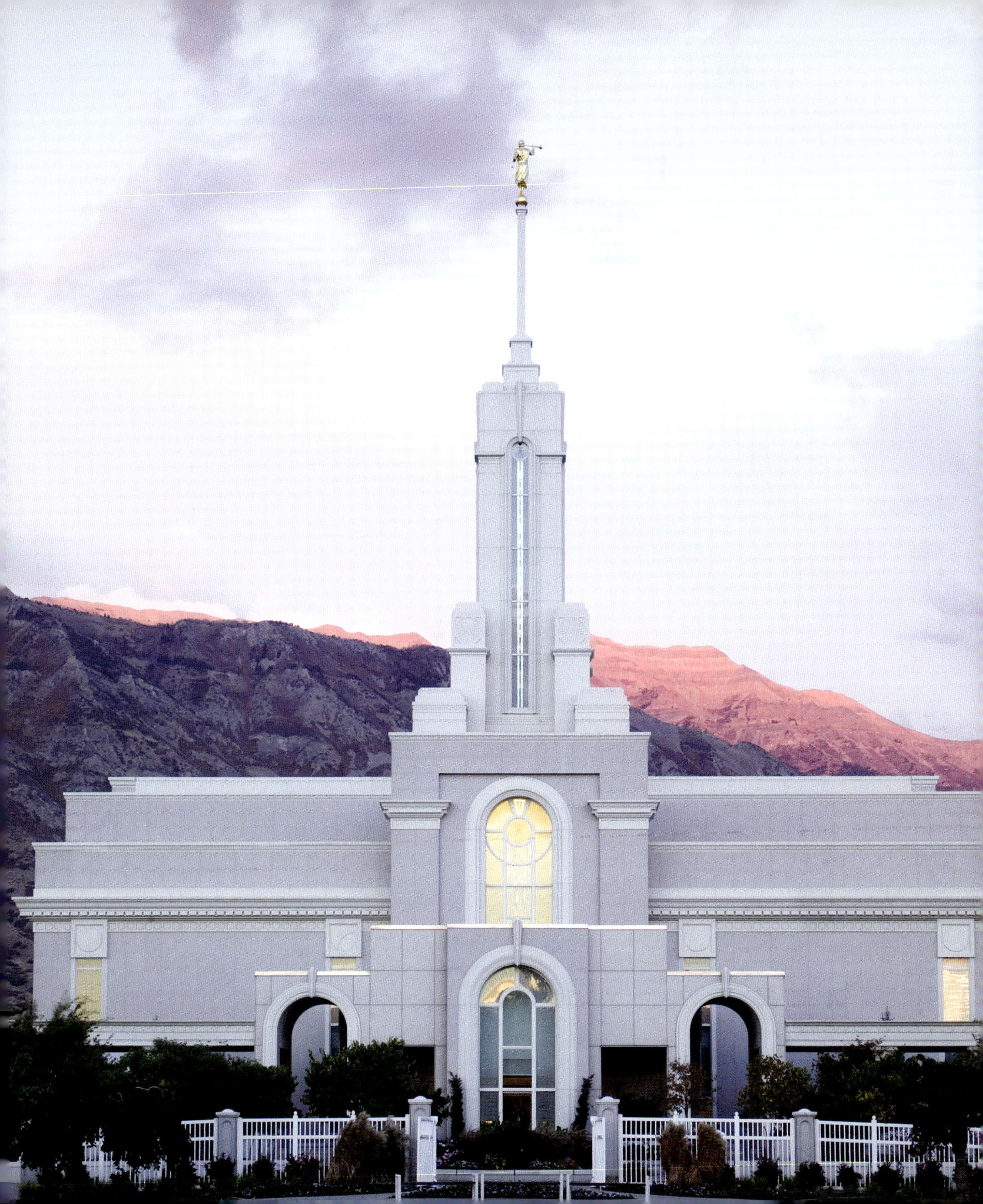

The Law of the Gospel and the Covenant

3 Nephi 11–25

Temple covenants make God's people peculiar, meaning that they become His own, or a special people (see Bible Dictionary, "peculiar"). By covenant, God consecrates His chosen people for singular assignment with responsibility to bring the blessings of the gospel to all of humanity. Connected to the covenant, God always attaches a requisite law that, if honored, instructs them in the principles of righteousness and helps them keep the covenant. At Mount Sinai, God invited the children of Israel to accept this type of peculiarity and responsibility. He announced, through Moses, that if they would "Obey my voice indeed, and keep my covenant, then ye shall be a peculiar treasure unto me above all people: for all the earth is mine: And ye shall be unto me a kingdom of priests, and an holy nation" (Exodus 19:5–6). At Sinai—Israel's early temple—God elected the Israelites to go through the ritual process of accepting the covenants and the law to which they were connected.[38] The Sinai pattern of election by covenant and law serves as a model to help us understand a similar experience for the Nephites, as well as the Latter-day Saint temple experience.

God began this process of consecrating Israel by calling seventy-three elders, including Aaron and two of his sons, Nadab and Abihu, to be the first to receive their ordinances on Mount Sinai preparatory to entering God's presence (see Exodus 24:1). Later these same elders were permitted to pass the veil of the holy cloud and enter the presence of God (see Exodus 24:9–11).[39]

The Joseph Smith Translation suggests that these seventy-three elders were not the only group of Israelites that God intended to endow with the higher blessings. It states that the first set of tablets, the one Moses broke, contained "the words of the everlasting covenant of the holy priesthood," the law with God's "holy order, and the ordinances thereof" (JST Deuteronomy 10:2; JST Exodus 34:1–2). In other words, the first set of tablets contained Melchizedek Priesthood teachings and temple ordinances that could ultimately bring Israel into God's presence to be taught and instructed by Him personally. Unfortunately, Israel as a whole rejected the fullness of these blessings through fear and disobedience. God, in His mercy, consequently gave Israel a lesser, preparatory set of statutes, taking away the law of the gospel and its ordinances but retaining Israel as His chosen people.[40] The second set of tablets did not have the Melchizedek Priesthood ordinances. It contained instead instructions on how to build

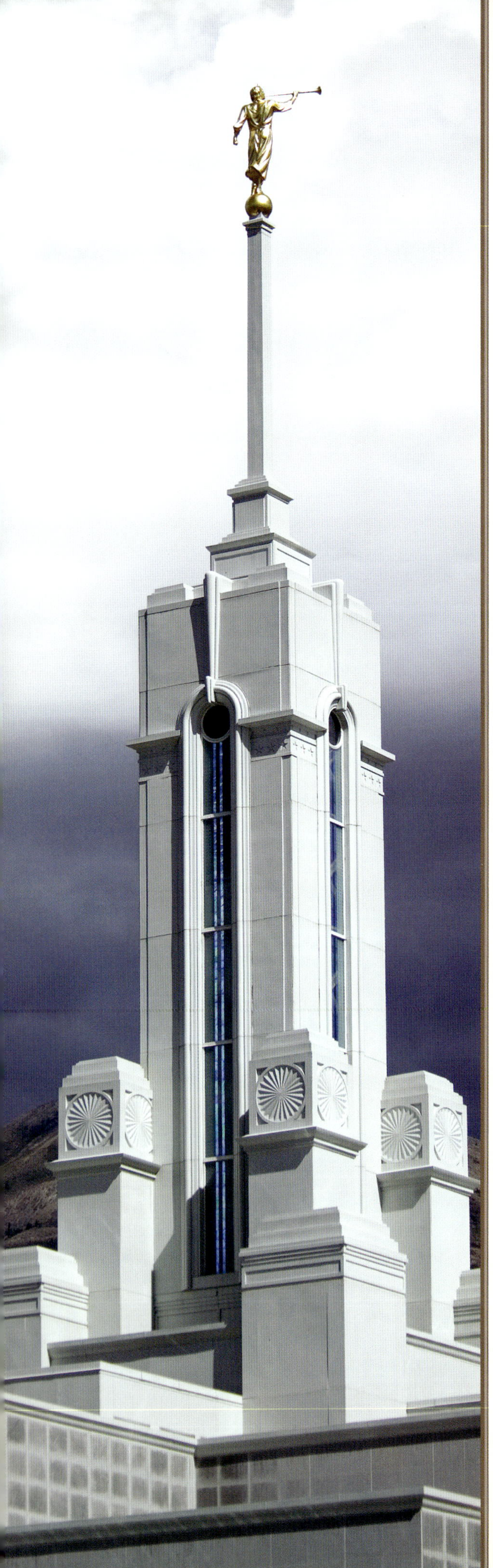

the Aaronic Priesthood temple of Moses, how to design the Aaronic Priesthood temple clothing, and how to perform the temple rites for the tabernacle. The Israelites also received commandments and ceremonies and requirements that would govern them and symbolically remind them that they must keep the covenant they were making with God. As the Bible Dictionary explains, "The law of Moses consisted of many ceremonies, rituals, and symbols, to remind the people frequently of their duties and responsibilities" ("Law of Moses").

The law of Moses was not a fullness of the gospel, but it was—let us not forget—still the foundation for the covenant that God would make with Israel to be His peculiar people. At Sinai, Israel agreed to abide by this preparatory law and accepted the covenant offered by God to be His peculiar people, announcing to Moses, "All the words which the Lord hath said will we do" (Exodus 24:3). To emphasize the importance of Israel's acceptance, Moses sprinkled the blood of oxen on them as a token of their covenant (see Exodus 24:3–8), possibly signifying the spiritual death that would result from the breaking of the covenant. The blood may also symbolize that the Atonement of Christ—made possible by the shedding of His blood—is always the center of the covenant that God makes with His chosen people.

After the original group of Israelites who had been delivered from Egypt had died out, God required the younger generation to renew the covenant. He told this newer group, through Moses, that the official renewal ceremony should take place under Joshua after they had entered the promised land, and He strongly cautioned them that if they did not honor the vows that they would make and keep His law, they would be punished and scattered among other nations (see Deuteronomy 27:1–13; 28:63–65). Mercifully and prophetically, Moses also promised Israel that if this happened—if the people rejected God and were scattered—God in His mercy would still eventually honor His covenant to make Israel His own, if and when they would repent, return unto the Lord, obey His law, and choose to be His peculiar people (see Deuteronomy 30:1–8). In scripture, this gathering, as we have seen, is a type and symbol of the redemption offered to all who repent and return to God.

We learn later that Israel, under the direction of Joshua, agreed to accept the law of Moses and the covenant to be God's peculiar people. They did so at an altar and in the presence of God, as represented by the ark of the covenant, verbally rehearsing the blessings and the penalties that would result respectively from obedience and disobedience (see Joshua 8:30–35). Just before Joshua's death, Israel again renewed the covenant, with themselves as witnesses that they had done so (see Joshua 24:14–28).

Unfortunately, the record of Israel's performance in keeping the law and its covenant is, as the Old Testament relates, generally dismal. Time and again, Israel followed after other gods. Consequently, Israel lost God's blessings, as promised, and was scattered in a several-hundred-year process of invasions and defeats by other nations. As a result, many generations of scattered Israelites have not had access to the great blessings promised by God to His covenant people and have not been able to perform their assignment to take the blessings of the gospel to the nations of the earth (see Abraham 2:11). However, the Book of Mormon makes it absolutely clear that God's covenant with Israel to make them His peculiar people is still binding. God will still choose all of the tribes of Israel for assignment and will restore to them His blessings as soon as they return to Him (see 2 Nephi 6:11; 10:7; 3 Nephi 29–33).

The Israelite pattern of election through covenant also appears in the Book of Mormon, but the requirements expected of the Nephites use the higher law as the foundation for the covenant. During His visit to the Nephites, Christ declared that the law of Moses was fulfilled in Him and that from that time forward He expected Israel to hold to what we would call the law of the gospel (see 3 Nephi 12:17–48). This new expectation astounded many of the Nephites who heard the Savior speak at the temple in Bountiful on the first day of His visit. They did not understand what He meant and wondered at His words about "old things" passing away (3 Nephi 15:2). Their wonderment should not be a big surprise. New innovations are seldom easy to accept for creatures of habit, as humans tend to be. Still, times and circumstances change, and,

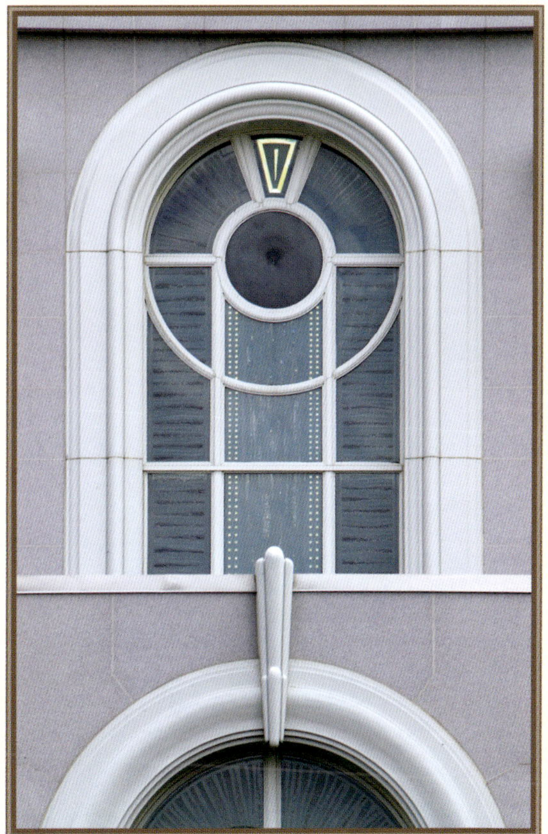

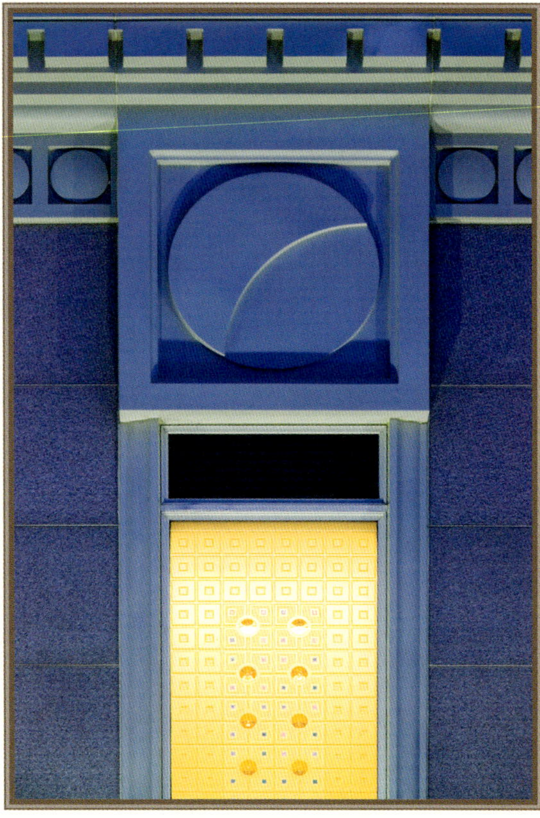

consequently, God can modify the particular details of religious ceremonies and rules and can require new expectations. Discerning the Nephites' confusion, Jesus explained that since He was the one who had given the law, He could also, therefore, change it. Most importantly, He made sure the Nephites knew that the covenant between God and Israel was still binding. He told them plainly, "the covenant which I have made with my people is not all fulfilled" (3 Nephi 15:4–8). Jesus admonished the Nephites to keep the commandments that He had just given them, saying that this was the law and the prophets (see 3 Nephi 15:10).

The account of God's election of the Nephites at Bountiful to go through the ritual process of accepting the new covenants and the new law is more subtle than the account with Israel in Exodus and Joshua, but nonetheless still discernible. Much, if not most, of the Savior's instruction to the Nephites during the first two days of His visit centered on the covenants. By the time He addressed their astonishment over the replacement of the law of Moses, for example, He had already taught them about and given them the authority to baptize (presumably the keys to the Aaronic Priesthood; see 3 Nephi 11:21–27). He had also already delivered the sermon at the temple, which John Welch has shown to be very much a covenant sermon.[41] In fact, Welch finds in this sermon, among other things, the laws of sacrifice and obedience (see 3 Nephi 12:19–20), chastity (see 3 Nephi 12:27–30), and consecration (see 3 Nephi 13:19–24), as well as the idea of the order of prayer (see 3 Nephi 13:9–15) and the idea that everyone must eventually be judged before they can enter into God's presence (see 3 Nephi 14:21–23). After the teachings about baptism and the sermon at the temple, and after He answered the question about fulfilling the law of Moses, the Savior then taught the disciples (see 3 Nephi 15:11–24; 16:1–20) about the covenant gathering of His sheep. Some time later that day, Christ gave the twelve disciples the power to confer the Holy Ghost (presumably the keys to the Melchizedek Priesthood; see 3 Nephi 18:37). He also, significantly, introduced the ordinance of the sacrament for all baptized members as a witness of their covenant to keep God's commandments (see 3 Nephi 18:10). All of this happened on the first day of the Savior's visit.

On the second day (see 3 Nephi 20–25), the Savior spent most of His time describing Israel's call as the chosen people, Israel's place in His plan for humankind, the Restoration and the Book of Mormon as signs for the beginning of the gathering of Israel through covenant, and the implications for individuals who have taken the covenants upon themselves. One of the most important

Mount Timpanogos Utah Temple

The Law of the Gospel and the Covenant

Both the east and west sides of the Mount Timpanogos Utah Temple promote the idea of ascension with steplike levels and rising towers. The architecture of this temple also includes the familiar figures of heavenly bodies—earth, moon, sun, and star stones, ascending in that order—to lift our eyes and souls heavenward to God and His celestial kingdom.

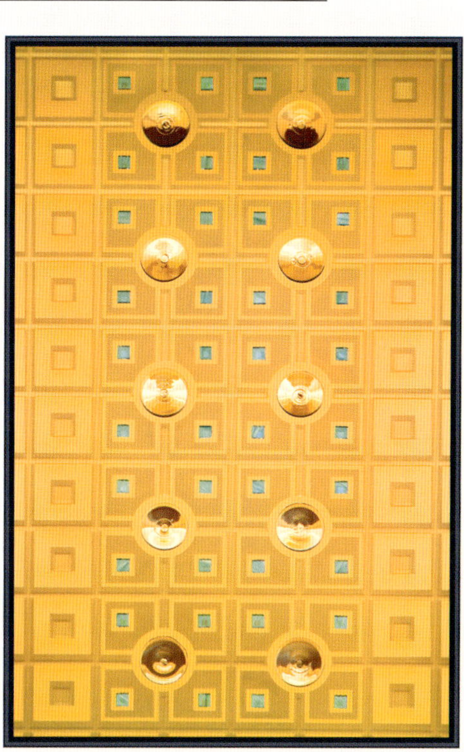

The final symbols that direct the human spirit upward are the tall rectangular windows capped with circles. These beautiful windows represent Jacob's ladder. The circle points to the celestial kingdom with steplike glass motifs proceeding up one side of the window and descending down the other. According to Keith Stepan, the architect, "there are plateaus" in the design of these beautiful windows "of man gaining a growth level as he seeks the influence of God. At the bottom is a pattern representing the earth."[42]

The idea and form of these windows is analogous to the rainbow that God gave to Noah as a token of His covenant. God told Noah that He would look upon the bow in the cloud as a sign of the covenant that He made with Enoch, and that conversely when Noah's posterity kept the commandments and looked upward to God, then Zion would look downward and the church of the first-born would come down from heaven and possess the earth (see JST Genesis 9:21–23). The simple magnificence of this symbol that ascends and descends from heaven to earth, like the symbolic windows of the Mount Timpanogos Temple, urges the Saints to remember God and honor the covenants they have made with Him.

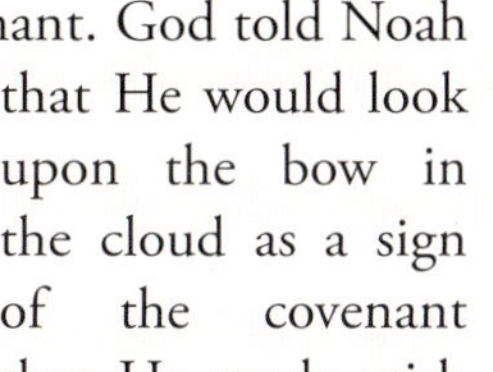

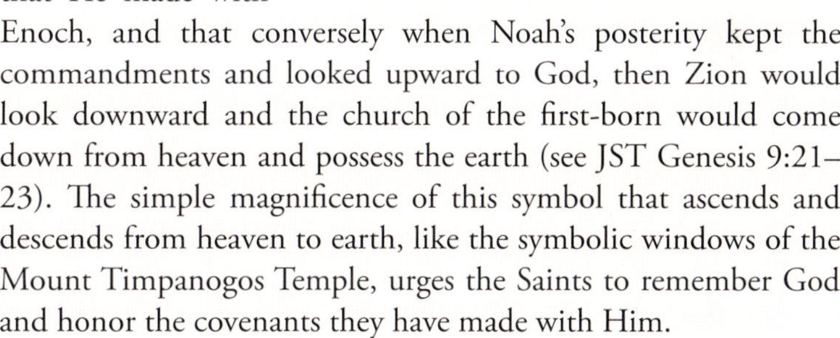

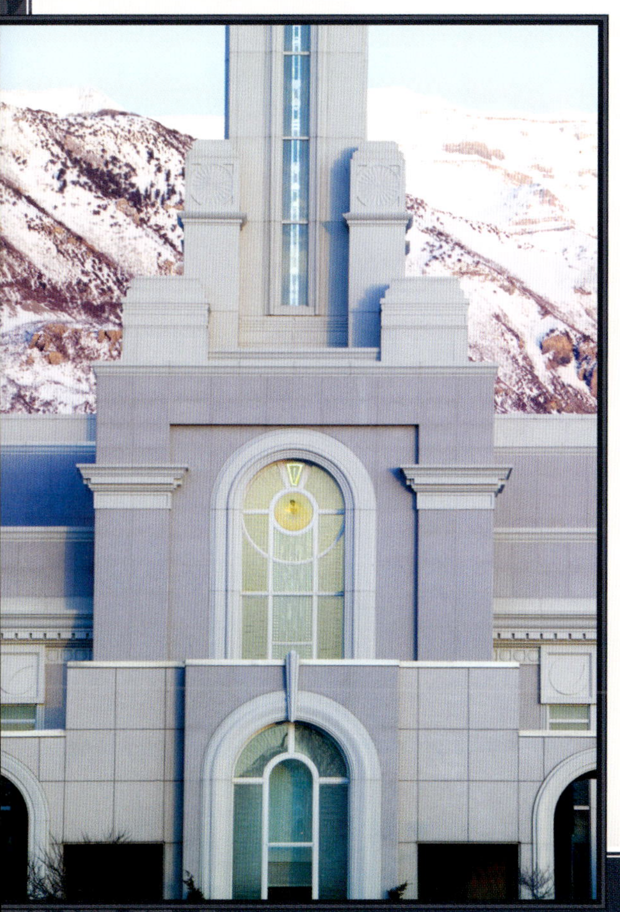

To keep the covenant, Latter-day Saints must keep the law of the gospel, which in essence is that when we do as God directs, He will be with us. The great reciprocal windows of the Mount Timpanogos Temple bear remarkable witness to this truth: we look to God for direction, and He looks to us to watch over us.

teachings on these issues is that if the people of the Gentile nations repent and listen to God, they will have God's church among them, come into the covenant, and be counted as Israelites (see 3 Nephi 21:22). As the Bible Dictionary puts it, "Those of non-Israelite lineage, commonly known as gentiles, are adopted into the house of Israel . . . through the ordinances of the gospel" ("Abraham, Covenant of"). Christ's final instructions of the second day, those concerning the return of Elijah, center squarely on the covenant but concern Latter-day Saints every bit as much as the Nephites and, in fact, require Latter-day revelations to understand.

The Elijah prophecy is part of Christ's quotation of the last two chapters of Malachi, which begin with the message that Christ, "the messenger of the covenant," will come again (Malachi 3:1; see also 3 Nephi 24:1). As part of the preparation for the Second Coming, Elijah will return. But for what purpose? The Bible/Book of Mormon version, to which Mormons and non-Mormons alike have easy access, gives only a partial answer. The Doctrine and Covenants/Pearl of Great Price version, which generally only Church members have read, reveals much more.

While the Bible/Book of Mormon version says that Elijah will come again (see Malachi 4:5; 3 Nephi 25:5), the "covenant-holding member" version relates that the foremost reason for Elijah's coming is to "reveal the Priesthood" (D&C 2:1). Latter-day prophets have explained that by "priesthood" Malachi means the highest of the Melchizedek Priesthood temple ordinances. President Ezra Taft Benson explains this idea in this way, drawing heavily from the teachings of Joseph Smith:

> What priesthood was Elijah to reveal? John the Baptist restored the keys to the Aaronic Priesthood. Peter, James, and John restored the keys of the kingdom of God. Why send Elijah?
>
> "Because he holds the keys of the authority to administer *in all the ordinances* of the priesthood," or the sealing power. (*Teachings,* p. 172; italics added.) So said the Prophet Joseph Smith!
>
> The Prophet Joseph said further that these keys were "the revelations, ordinances, oracles, powers and endowments of the *fulness of the Melchizedek Priesthood* and of the kingdom of God on the earth." (*Teachings,* p. 337; italics added.) [43]

Given President Benson's definition of what Elijah revealed, the understanding of the second difference in the "covenant" version of the prophecy also becomes clearer. Malachi 4:6 (see also 3 Nephi 25:6) says that Elijah will "turn the heart of the fathers to the children, and the heart of the children to their fathers." The "covenant" version changes that statement, declaring that Elijah will "plant in the hearts of the children the promises made to the fathers" (D&C 2:2). The fathers are the patriarchs—Abraham, Isaac, and Jacob. The promises made to them are the temple covenants. Small wonder that the promises of the fathers should be planted in the hearts of the children: the promises are the covenants that lead to exaltation, and the children are the Latter-day Saints whose hearts will yearn after these temple blessings.

The Bible Dictionary explains that we receive the promises of exaltation just as the great patriarchs did—by temple covenant:

> Abraham first received the gospel by baptism (which is the covenant of salvation). Then he had conferred upon him the higher priesthood, and he entered into celestial marriage (which is the covenant of exaltation),

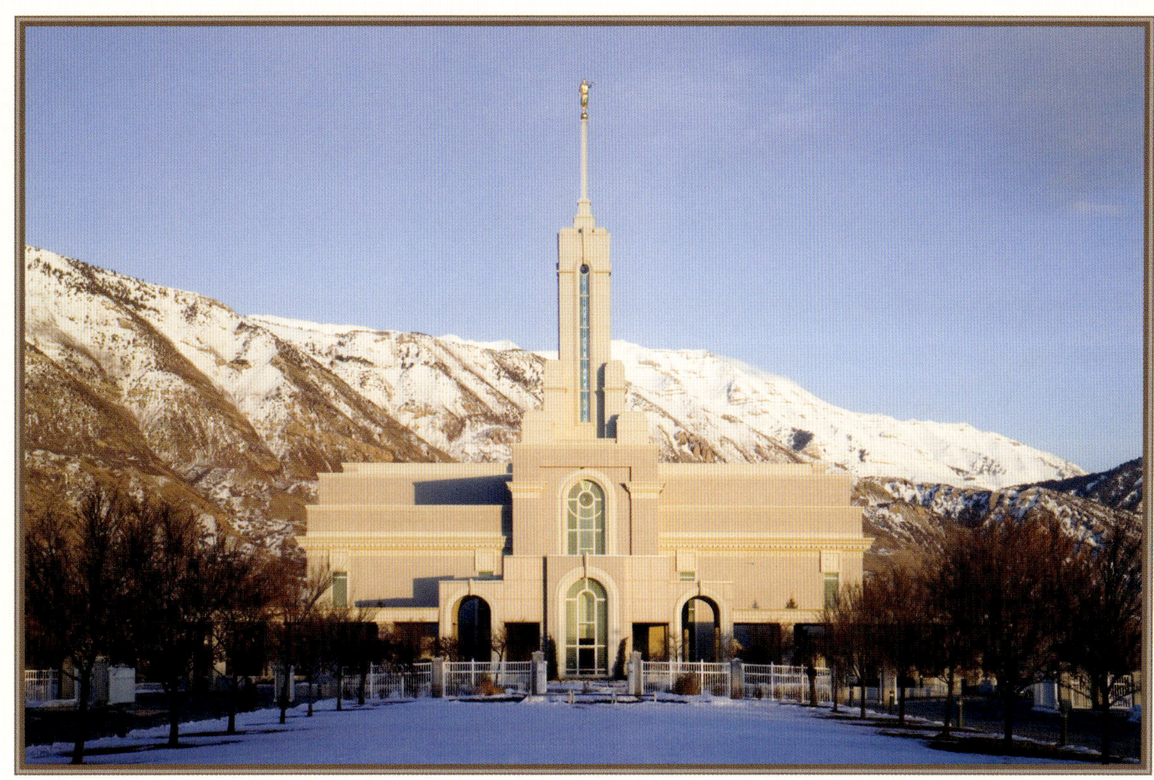

gaining assurance thereby that he would have eternal increase. . . . The portions of the covenant that pertain to personal salvation and eternal increase are renewed with each individual who receives the ordinance of celestial marriage. ("Abraham, Covenant of.")

Once they have received their own temple blessings, Latter-day Saints will obviously be anxious to help their departed ancestors receive their blessings. The "covenant" version therefore, prophesies that after the Latter-day Saints have received their own blessings, their "hearts will turn to their fathers" (D&C 2:2). In other words, knowing the worth of their own covenants, Latter-day Saints will desire to find their ancestors through genealogical work and then have their ancestors' temple work done vicariously in temples.

Finally, the "covenant" version declares that if Elijah did not restore these keys to the temple ordinances that make exaltation possible, the whole Creation would have been a waste (see D&C 2:3). The purpose of the Creation was, after all, to provide a place of testing so that God could exalt His children. The keys that Elijah restored are the last factor in the process of exaltation. Without those keys, exaltation would not be possible and the purpose for the Creation of the earth would be unfulfilled.

For modern Israel, Christ's teachings to the Nephites have special significance. God has once again called Israel to Sinai, so to speak. The law of the gospel has been restored. The covenants of baptism and the temple ordinances that consecrate Israel as God's chosen people with responsibility have been restored. The keys necessary to make Israel's election sure so that they can have exaltation have been restored. God has remembered His covenant to gather Israel, and the process has begun. It happens in the temple.

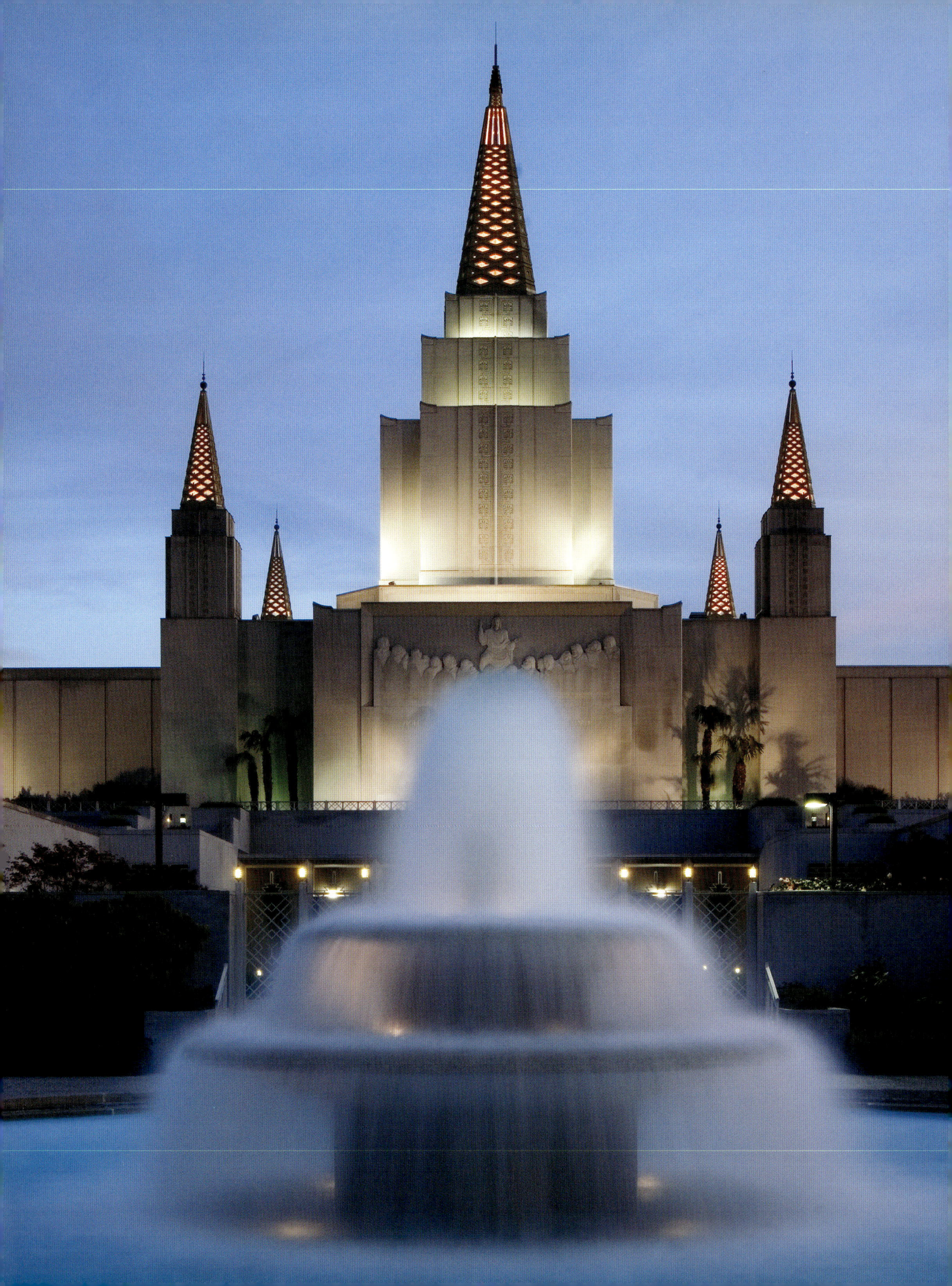

Entering the Presence of God

The Book of Ether

Temples prepare God's children to see Him (in this life or the next) and to be taught by Him. Temple covenants train Latter-day Saints in the ways of righteousness and, therefore, make this miracle possible. If the Saints maintain faith in God's promises and keep their covenants, Christ will come unto them, as He declares in the book of Ether, and "show unto [them] the greater things, the knowledge which is hid up because of unbelief" (Ether 4:13). No place in scripture bears stronger testimony of this marvelous possibility than the book of Ether. This great book does two things. It witnesses throughout that righteous men and women can gain the faith necessary to see God, and it uses the "good/evil contrast" pattern to emphasize the surety of this possibility.

The record begins with a rather long account of how the brother of Jared is led by God to enter His presence. More than a quarter of the verses of the book of Ether—115 out of 433—are dedicated to this one event. So much emphasis on a single occurrence in an abridgment that summarizes hundreds of years of history (in roughly just another 261 verses[44]) indicates that the message of this story will set the tone for the rest of the book. Indeed, the entire book is dominated by the pattern of this one story, ably analyzed by gospel scholar Catherine Thomas. Thomas notes that the brother of Jared is tested on a long journey, calls upon the name of the Lord, is brought to a cloud-veil where he sees the hand of God, is brought through faith into the presence of God, and is taught marvelous things that are sacred and must be sealed up.[45] After showing us this pattern, Moroni announces that this experience does not have to be unique to the brother of Jared. He encourages his modern readers to know that they also, through faith, can receive the same revelations (see Ether 4:7). He lends greater credibility to this possibility with two more witnesses, first reporting later in the Jaredite history how Emer also saw the Son of Righteousness (see Ether 9:22), and then bearing his own testimony that he himself has seen Jesus (see Ether 12:39).

These three examples of men seeing God, placed toward the beginning, center, and end of the abridgment, function as a startling contrast to the rest of the book, a record that chronicles the gross wickedness and wars running throughout Jaredite history. They show that it is possible, even in an immoral society, for righteous individuals to develop the necessary faith to "rend that veil of unbelief," as Moroni puts it (Ether 4:15), and enter into God's presence. The skeletal approach of Moroni's abridgment stresses this message. Rather than flesh out

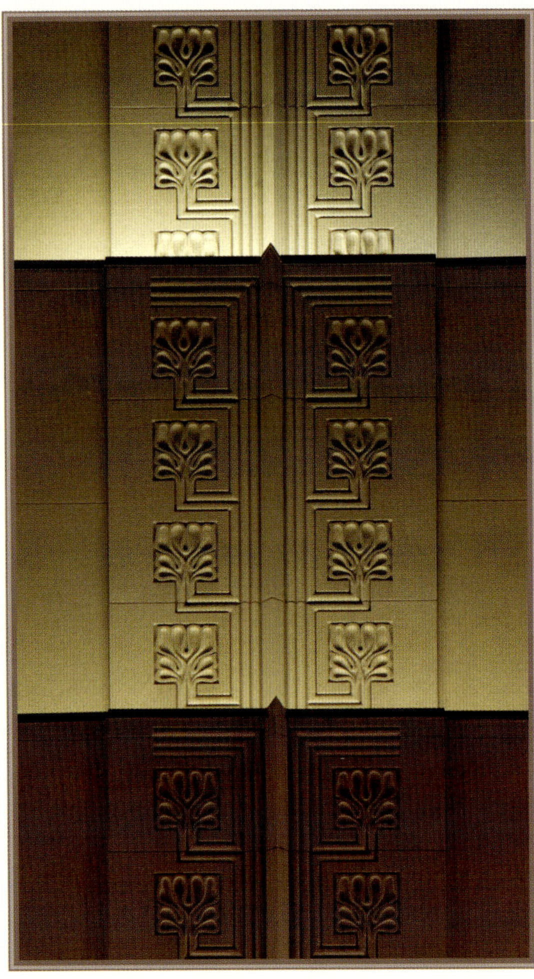

the characterization of any particular person or persons in a multi-hundred-year history, Moroni provides minimal detail on people, highlighting instead, in stark, fast-paced, and sequential fashion, stories about the secret combinations of the Jaredites. By interspersing this sinister history with examples of individuals who passed the trial of faith and received their sure witness of God, Moroni encourages any who desire righteousness to move forward in faith, no matter how evil the wickedness that surrounds them.

The secret combinations of the Jaredites were perniciously evil—so evil that in many cases sons plotted to kill or imprison their fathers, and brothers plotted the same against brothers. They formed these combinations to obtain and promote positions of power and wealth, which Moroni suggests are almost always the motivation for secret combinations. He indicates that the secret combinations were the cause of the destruction of both the Jaredites and the Nephites and that these combinations occur among all people (see Ether 8:20–22).

Secret combinations occur on many levels and in many forms—drug gangs, colluding companies, organized crime, bullies in junior high schools—but they always unite wicked people and forces and for this reason are particularly difficult to battle. The battle is challenging enough for the organized forces of righteousness. For individuals, the battle can seem overwhelming and requires great faith. So difficult is this struggle between good and evil that the book of Revelation portrays it as a struggle between a lamb and a beast. The lamb has twelve horns (see JST Revelation 5:6), representing the priesthood power of the Apostles, and the beast has ten horns, representing the different forces that join together to create one terrifying monster. The general attitude of many in the world toward this awe-inspiring beast manifests itself in the question asked by most people: "Who is able to make war with [the beast]?" (Revelation 13:4). These people often fear that the beast is invincible, leading them to say, "If you can't beat 'em, join 'em." But John says that the "patience and the faith of the saints" (Revelation 13:10) protects them from this evil. They have faith that the lamb will eventually defeat the beast, so they refuse to join with the beast.

For followers of Christ, this metaphor of the lamb's victory over the beast carries immense symbolic significance. Normally, only a fool would bet on a lamb in a fight against a beast. But that is exactly the level of faith that God requires of His true disciples.

The Lamb's victory must be purchased with His own sacrifice and death—Gethsemane, Golgotha, and the tomb—before He conquers by means of the Resurrection. Likewise, if the Lamb's followers would gain victory over the beast, they must also live the law of sacrifice and give their lives—"whosoever will save his life shall lose it: and whosoever will lose his life for my sake shall find it" (Matthew 16:25)—before they gain victory by being reborn. Put more simply, Christ's true followers must offer themselves to God. They must sacrifice a broken heart and contrite spirit (see 3 Nephi 9:20). They must give up the desires of the natural man and seek instead to submit perfectly to God's will with faith that God will honor His promises and give them exaltation.

This level of faith is the theme of Moroni's greatest editorial in the book of Ether. Moroni begins with what is now his well-known statement that "ye receive no witness until after the trial of your faith" (Ether 12:6). This can be understood on many levels, but it seems clear from the rest of the editorial that Moroni particularly meant the highest kind of witness—that no one could see God and be taught by Him personally without being well-trained and well-tested. The reason for this trial is that God cannot give His children His knowledge, and thus His power, until He has educated them to use it for only His righteous purposes. Faith in the face of adversity is the tool that God uses to tutor His children.

True faith unto salvation means trusting God at His word. It means having confidence that following His revelatory instructions will lead us to develop godlike character; we trust that the sacrifices He requires of us will make us like Him. In the process of obeying His counsel, we learn to use godly powers wisely. Only if we have this type of faith will God grant us His power to perform

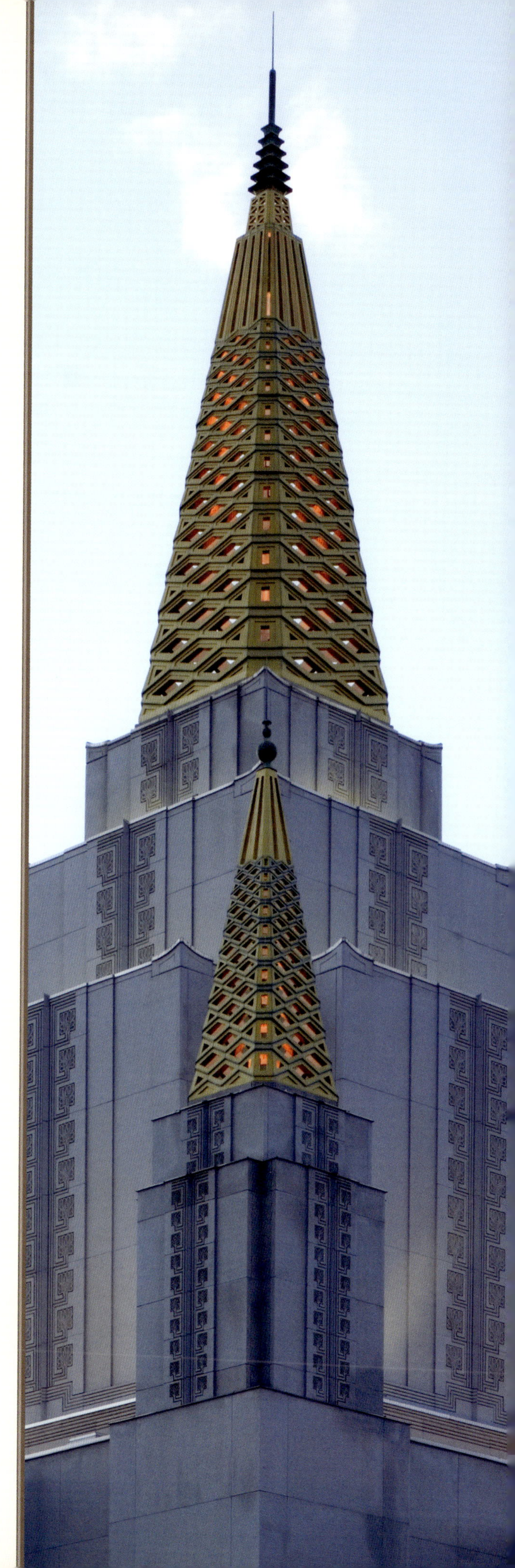

Oakland California Temple

The Presence of God

Dominating its surroundings, the Oakland California Temple testifies that God invites all of His children to come into His presence. The most striking symbolic features on the Oakland California Temple are the two friezes of Christ teaching His people. On the north frieze, the Savior teaches His followers in the Holy Land. The south frieze portrays Christ teaching the Nephites. Many levels of meaning could be derived from the friezes, but at their most essential level they remind all temple attendees that the Lord's house prepares them to stand in God's presence and be taught. This is the grand purpose of the Melchizedek Priesthood.

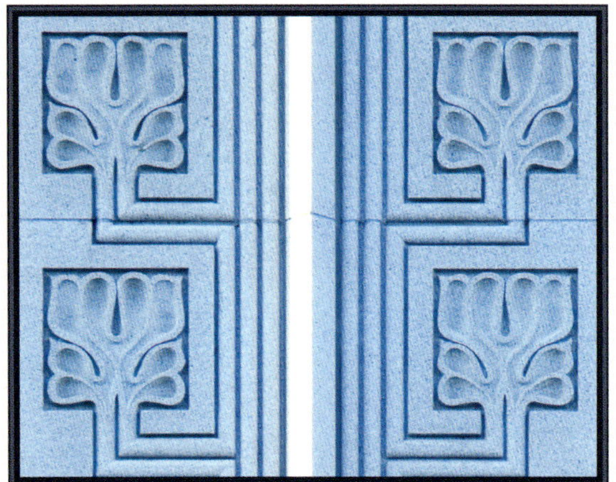

Doctrine and Covenants 84:19–24 declares that the keys to the knowledge of God and the power of godliness are held by the Melchizedek Priesthood and that by receiving the ordinances of the Melchizedek Priesthood—the temple ordinances—the Saints become eligible to receive the power of godliness and to see God face-to-face. These verses even indicate that God intended to give these blessings to ancient Israel, but Israel rejected them. It is only after the trial of faith that these blessings can be received, as Moroni states (see Ether 12:6–19), and Israel could not muster the faith to receive them. For most Latter-day Saints, the trial of faith is the long journey of mortal life, and the entrance into the presence of God will occur in eternity, not mortality. But it is this blessing, nevertheless, that the Saints must hope for and work toward.

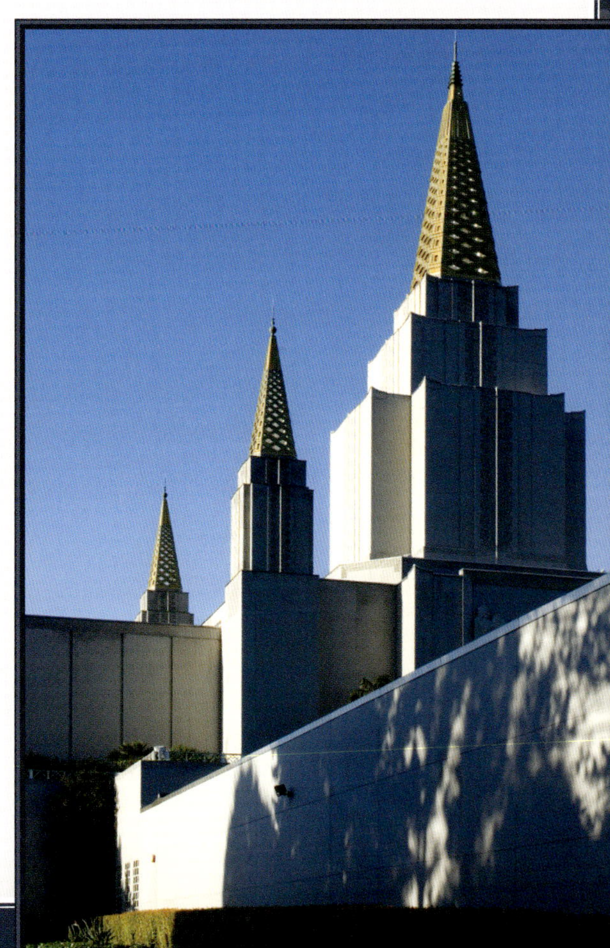

Three additional familiar symbols contribute to the Oakland Temple's overall theme of entering the presence of God—the great spires, the ascending towers, and the tree of life motif. The tree of life motif appears on each side of the ascending towers leading to the spires, reminding Latter-day Saints of Lehi's endowment journey into God's presence. As always, the spires raise our sight to God and encourage us to aspire to His character. The ascending towers likewise lift our gaze toward heaven and remind us that our goal is to live worthy of being welcomed there for eternity.

These four powerful symbols—the friezes of God's presence, the tree of life motif, the spires, and the ascending towers—inspire the Saints to seek the one thing that matters most, to be taught personally by God the mysteries of His godliness.

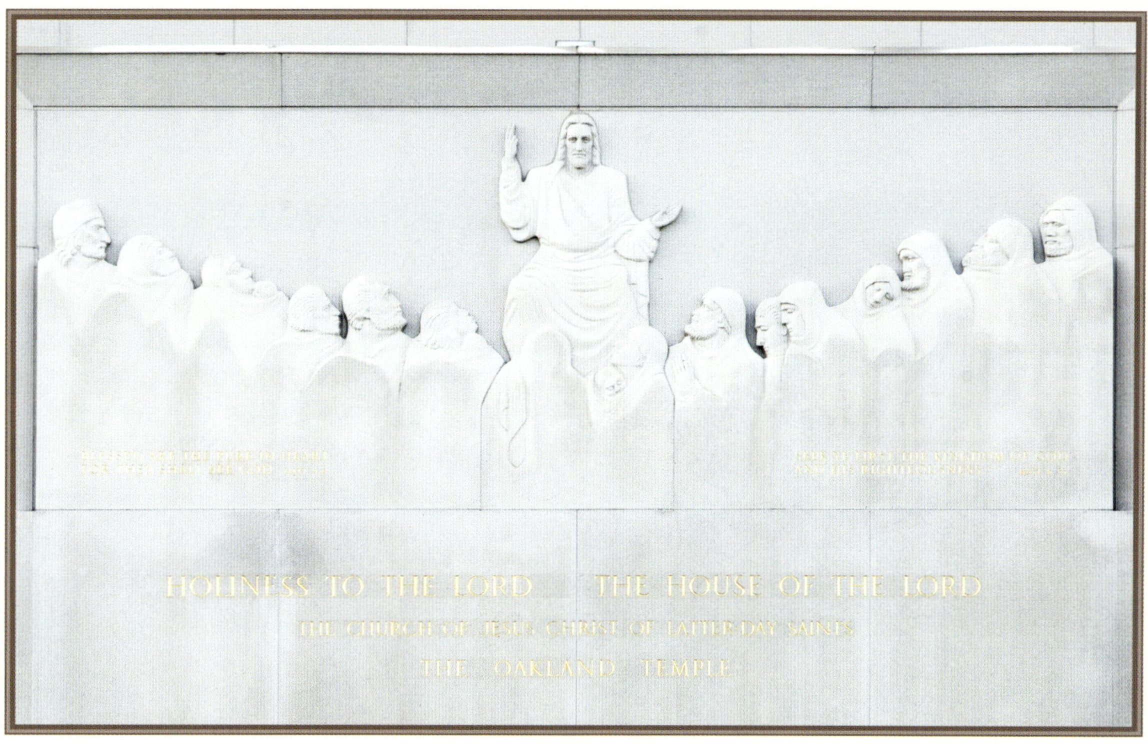

miracles. Moroni's long list of people who had such power testifies to and portrays examples of this salvational principle. He relates, for instance, that the law of Moses was given only by faith; that Alma and Amulek brought down the prison walls of Ammonihah by faith; that Nephi and Lehi, and later Ammon, converted thousands of Lamanites by faith; and that the three Nephite disciples by faith obtained a promise that they would not taste of death (see Ether 12:11–17). Most spectacularly, Moroni announces that proven men and women can see God personally, declaring that Christ showed Himself to the Nephites after His Resurrection because of their faith (see Ether 12:7). He states categorically that God does not show Himself to any people until after their faith has been proven (see Ether 12:12). Finally, referring back to the supreme illustration of his abridgment, Moroni states that there were many, the brother of Jared in particular, who could not be kept without the veil before Jesus came in mortality, who saw Christ through faith (see Ether 12:19–21).

The doctrine is clear. God expects His Saints to live lives of sufficient faith and purity that they can be taught by Him in His presence.[46] What is taught by God in this experience is less clear, though the scriptures do yield some insights. According to Moroni, the brother of Jared saw "all the inhabitants of the earth which had been, and also all that would be" (Ether 3:25). Not much more is said, but this little bit sounds similar to the vision that Moses had (see Moses 1:8, 27–29). We know that the brother of Jared's vision is similar to what John saw in the book of Revelation because Moroni tells us that this is so (see Ether 4:16), and we know, according to Joseph Smith, that John's vision was a Second Comforter experience:

> When any man obtains this last Comforter, he will have the personage of Jesus Christ to attend him, or appear unto him from time to time,

> and even He will manifest the Father unto him, and they will take up their abode with him, and the visions of the heavens will be opened unto him, and the Lord will teach him face to face, and he may have a perfect knowledge of the mysteries of the Kingdom of God; and this is the state and place the ancient Saints arrived at when they had such glorious visions—Isaiah, Ezekiel, John upon the Isle of Patmos, St. Paul in the three heavens, and all the Saints who held communion with the general assembly and Church of the Firstborn.[47]

Nephi also had this same experience. He tells us that his vision of the tree of life, though differently described, was the same vision that John the Revelator received (see 1 Nephi 14:18–27). Trained and tested and found faithful, Isaiah, Ezekiel, John, Paul, Nephi, and the brother of Jared were taught on a level that could only be presented by God Himself. According to Moroni, the things these men saw can only be revealed to those who have repented and been sanctified in Christ and have shown the type of faith that they had shown. To all others, these things are sealed until they also prove by faith and repentance that they can righteously use the knowledge and power of God (see Ether 4:6–7). Though reading the shortened versions of the visions of the individuals above might give us a glimpse of their content, the fullness of the teachings must come from God Himself.

Unlikely as it is that most of us will have the Second Comforter experience in this life, seeking the face of God is, nonetheless, exactly what Moroni exhorts us to pursue. It is, in fact, the theme of his abridgment of the Jaredite records. Twice, at the most

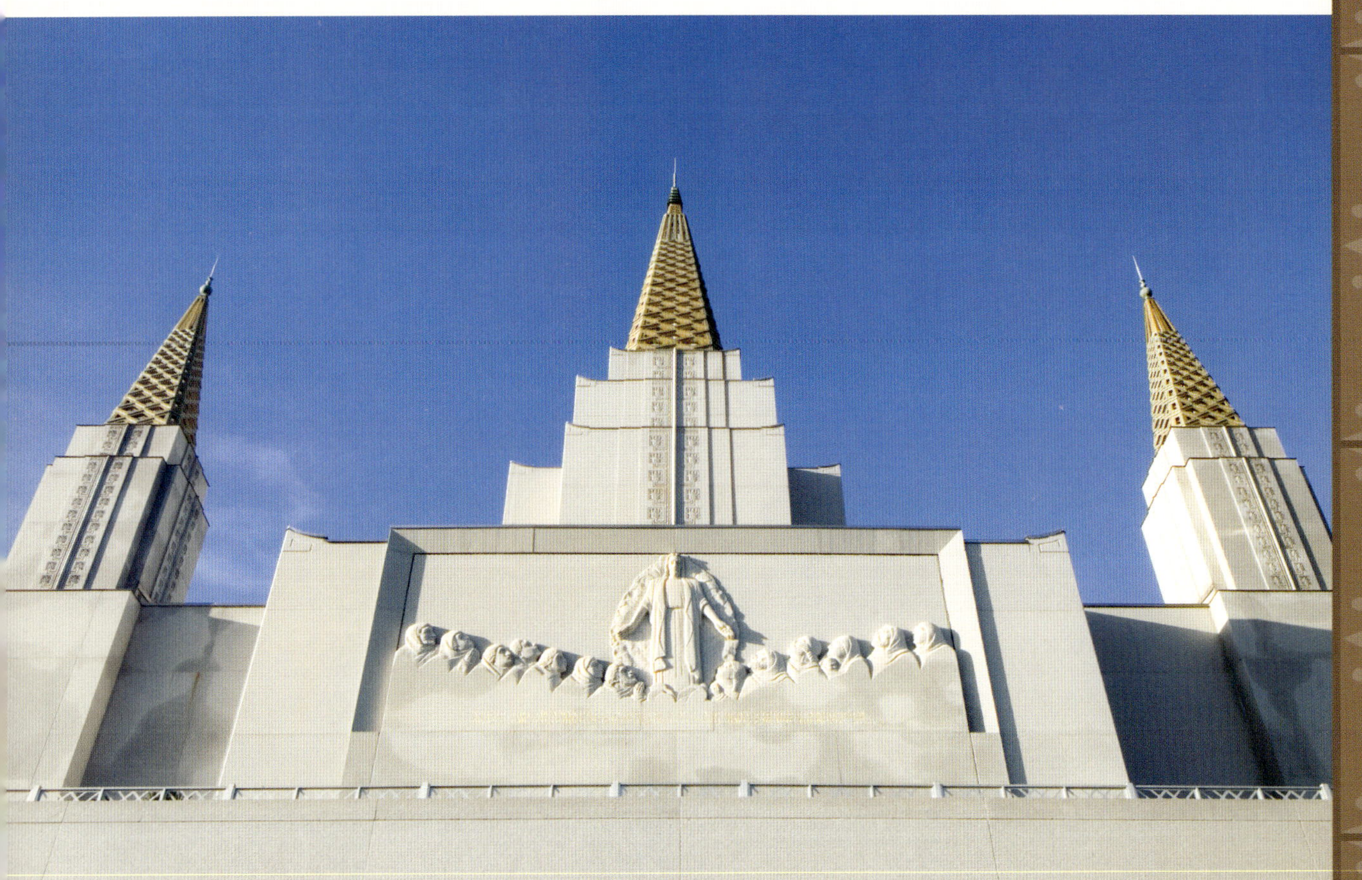

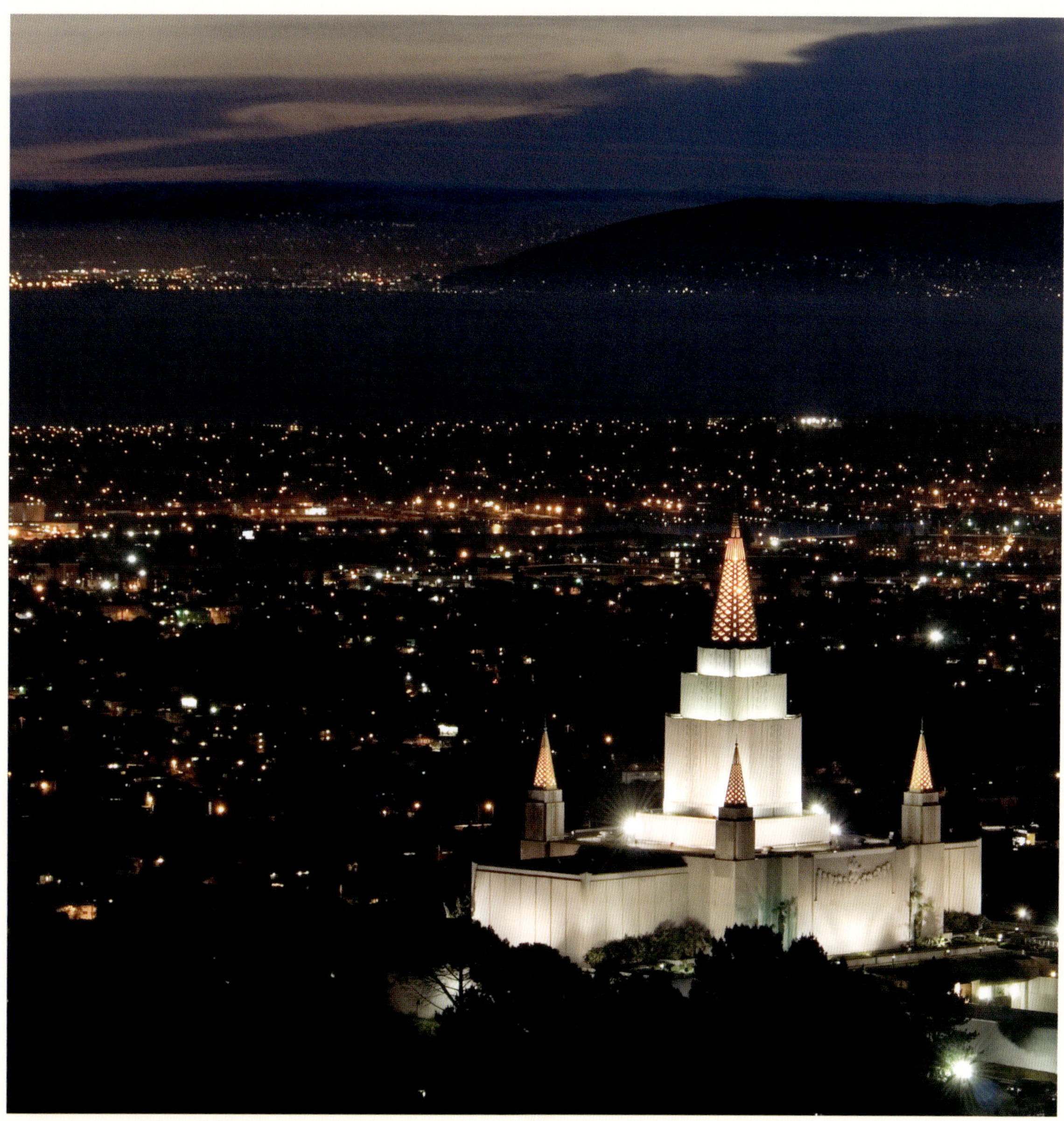

pivotal points in the book, he challenges us to know God and learn from Him. In the first challenge he quotes Christ, saying, "Come unto me, O ye Gentiles, and I will show unto you the greater things, the knowledge which is hid up because of unbelief" (Ether 4:13). The second challenge follows Moroni's own witness that he has personally seen the Lord. He says, "And now, I would commend you to seek this Jesus of whom the prophets and apostles have written" (Ether 12:41). For Moroni, seeing the face of God seems to be his great point of encouragement for his readers. He knows that God-fearing mortal human beings can develop the faith, even in the midst of a wicked world, to pass through the veil, see the face of God, and be taught by Him. His abridgment of the Jaredite history shows that this is true. The modern endowment helps us understand this goal. It shows us the patterns for the search. It teaches us the conditions by which the task can be accomplished and places us under covenant to keep those conditions. It endows us with the necessary gifts and encourages us to use them.

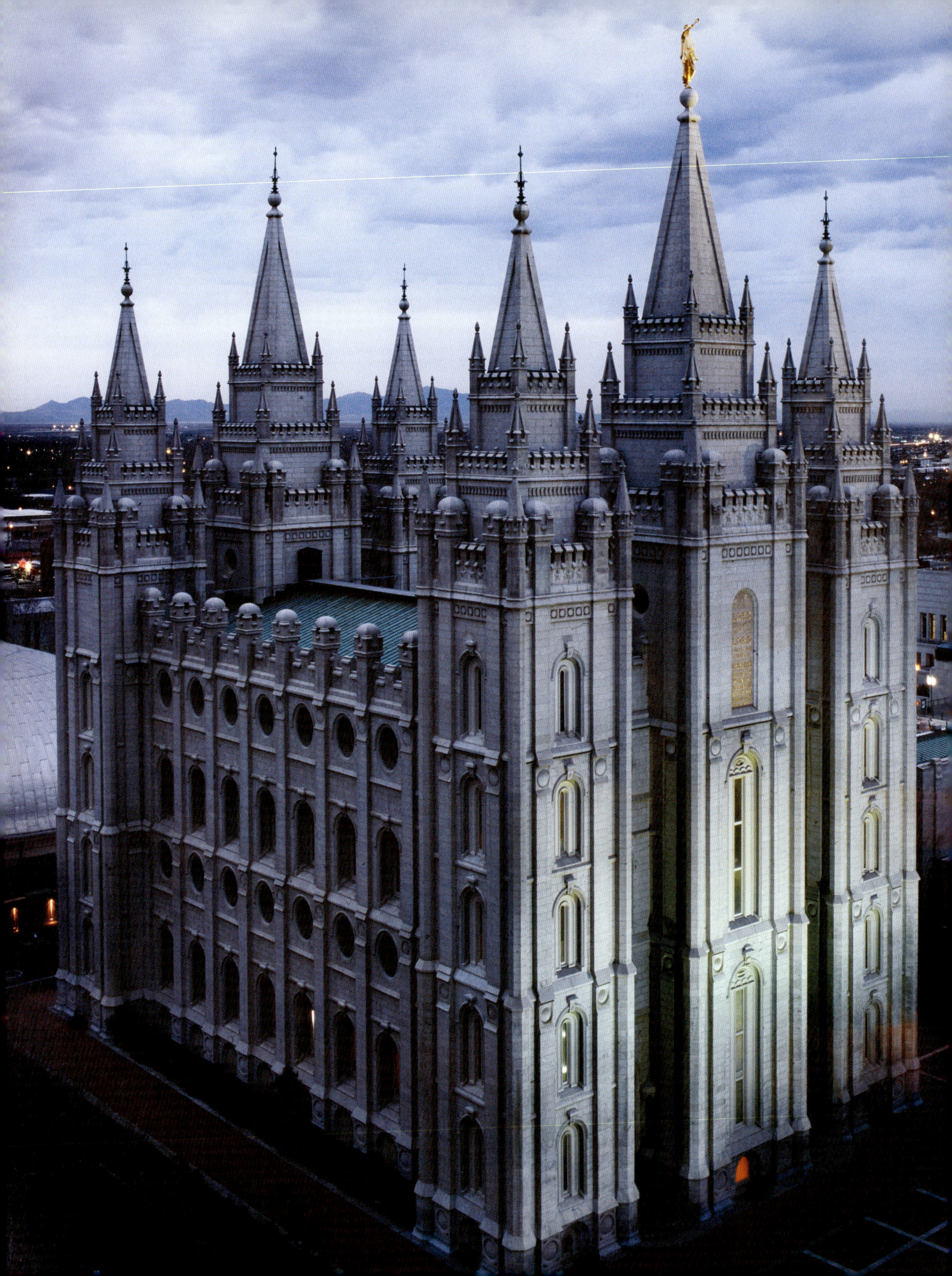

THE GIFTS OF GOD

MORONI 10

In this final chapter, we will imitate Moroni in the last chapter of the Book of Mormon and give a reminder of the mercies and gifts that God offers to His children. The chapter will have a temple emphasis, but it is more a statement of gratitude for the temple than it is an examination of specific symbols or doctrines.

About thirty-six years after the destruction of his people at the battle of Cumorah, Moroni made ready to seal up the plates. He alone among the Nephites had escaped the Lamanites who hunted the last remaining members of that society (see Mormon 8:2–3). He had, at some point in time, seen the three Nephite disciples (see Mormon 8:11) and the Savior (see Ether 12:39), but this probably did not occur often enough to alleviate the tremendous loneliness he must have experienced. He evidently did some writing during this period because on two occasions he mentions dates that are after the battle of Cumorah (see Mormon 8:6; Moroni 10:1). We can assume that he abridged the book of Ether sometime during these thirty-six years. We know that he had to keep himself alive and provisioned, so he had labors to occupy his time. Nevertheless, we can still suppose that he had enormous amounts of time to ponder the important things of life and eternity.

Presumably, the last thing a prophet would write in a book of scripture before sealing it up for more than a thousand years would be of tremendous value. To say the least, his final written words would be worthy of strict and close attention, and should be read with great anticipation of what he might choose to emphasize in his last witness. With this in mind, we read with deep appreciation that Moroni chose to emphasize the mercies and gifts of God in his last testimony.

Moroni's choice to emphasize God's mercy is astounding given the long history of the Nephites. The account of the continual slide of the Nephites into pride and wickedness that seems ever present, as well as the fact that their wickedness leads to their destruction, might cause one to believe that Moroni would end his record with a fearful warning of God's justice and the sure damnation that awaits those who do not repent. Instead, he leaves us with a testimony of God's love and the potential that each of us has to come to Christ and be made perfect through His grace. When combined, the eight exhortations (see Moroni 10:3, 4, 8, 18, 19, 24–27, 30–33) powerfully witness that God is merciful and full of grace and that He will make us holy through the shedding of the blood of Christ if we reject all ungodliness and do not deny his power (see Moroni 10:32–33).

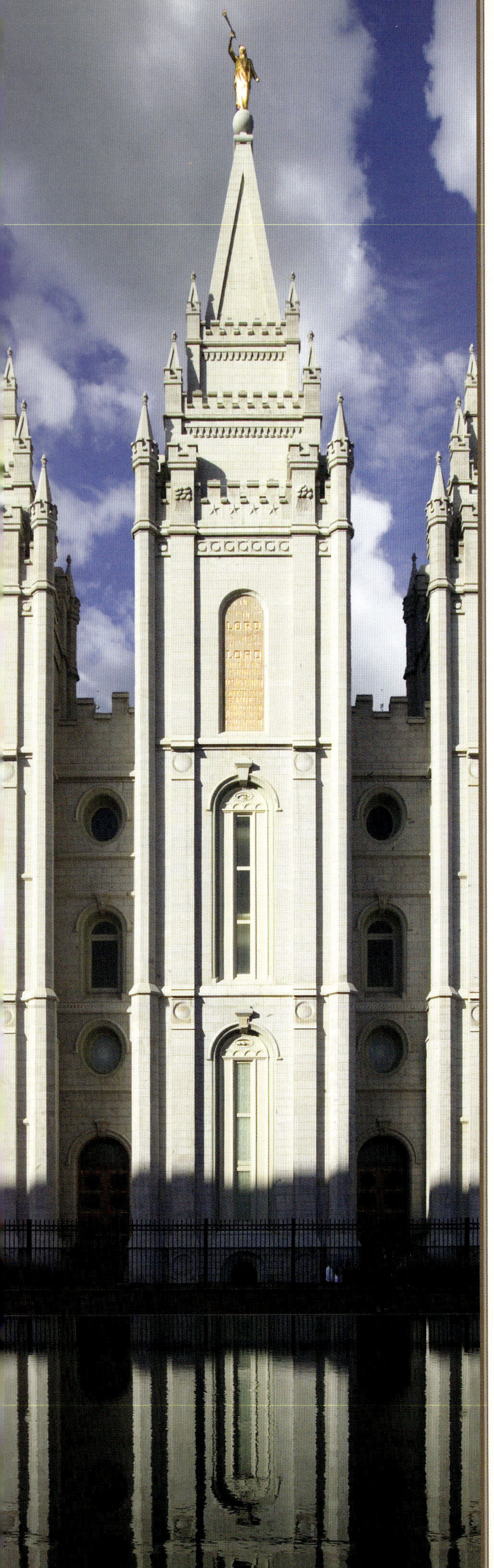

In the first of the eight exhortations, Moroni sets the tone and establishes the theme for the following seven. He tells us that as we read the Book of Mormon we should "remember how merciful the Lord hath been unto the children of men," throughout the history of the world, "and ponder it in [our] hearts" (Moroni 10:3). While there are many useful ways to read the Book of Mormon, reading it with an emphasis on God's mercies may be the most powerful. It should give us the strength and faith to keep going in a lone and dreary world and provide us with hope that the long journey will be worth the effort. It should encourage us to have charity for others out of gratitude for our own remission of sins. Nephi told us in the beginning of the Book of Mormon in what amounts to his thesis statement that we should read the book in this way: "I, Nephi, will show unto you that the tender mercies of the Lord are over all those whom he hath chosen, because of their faith, to make them mighty even unto the power of deliverance" (1 Nephi 1:20). It appears to be more than coincidental that in the end of the book, Moroni recapitulates and highlights Nephi's thesis.

In exhortation number two, Moroni admonishes us to read the Book of Mormon and to ask God if these things are not true. I believe by the term *these things* he is particularly asking us to pray concerning the truths concerning the mercy of God as they are defined in the Book of Mormon. His counsel to pray can obviously refer to other principles in the Book of Mormon and to the truthfulness of the book itself. But the context of the chapter suggests that God's mercy may be Moroni's primary concern. After this admonishment, Moroni declares that if we read and ask sincerely in faith, God will confirm the truth of these things to us by the power of the Holy Ghost (see Moroni 10:4).

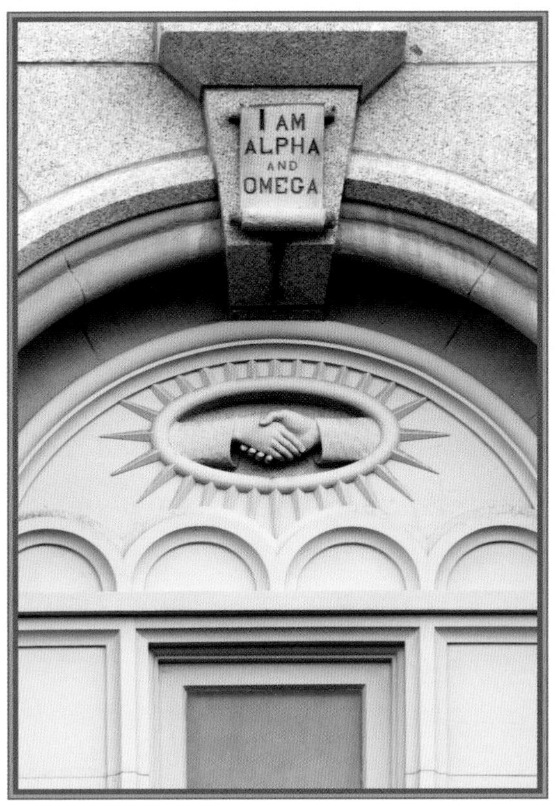

In exhortation three (see Moroni 10:7), Moroni declares that we must not deny the power of God, clearly admonishing us, at the very least, to have faith in God's ability to forgive us and sanctify us. It is one of Satan's best tactics to make us believe that God cannot or will not forgive us. Moroni's third exhortation should convince us to see through Satan's lie.

Exhortation four encourages us to not deny the gifts of God (see Moroni 10:8–17). It explains that there are many heavenly gifts and that all of them come from God for the benefit of His children. It contains a list of gifts that includes such things as healing, working miracles, beholding angels, and the gift of tongues and seems to imply that if God can give such marvelous things to mortal men and women, then forgiving them and sanctifying His children is something that God can and wants to do.

The fifth exhortation (see Moroni 10:18) is a follow-up to the fourth and confirms that all good gifts come of Christ, recalling to our minds that He did, indeed, atone, die, and resurrect for us so that we might partake of God's mercies.

Exhortation six (see Moroni 10:19–23) begins with Moroni's testimony that God does not change, that His gifts are available to all people at all times, and that only through unbelief are the gifts withheld. He then explains that we must have faith in God's gifts, that this faith in the gifts always leads to hope and charity, and that if we do not have faith, hope, and charity then we cannot be saved. Under such circumstances, he declares, we would be in despair.

In the seventh exhortation (see Moroni 10:24–29), Moroni exhorts us to remember what he has said, remember that the gifts of God are given through a belief that God will give them, and that we cannot be saved without them.

In his eighth and last exhortation (see Moroni 10:30–33), Moroni entreats us to come unto Christ and accept His gifts, to be

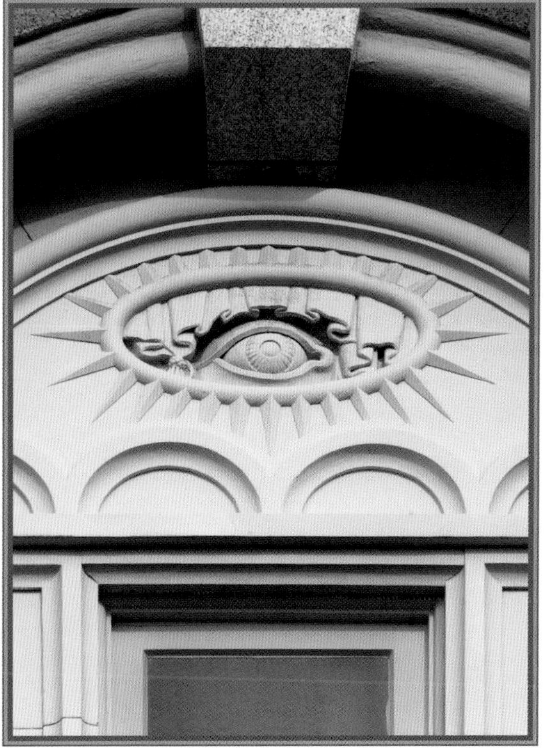

Salt Lake Utah Temple

The Gifts of God

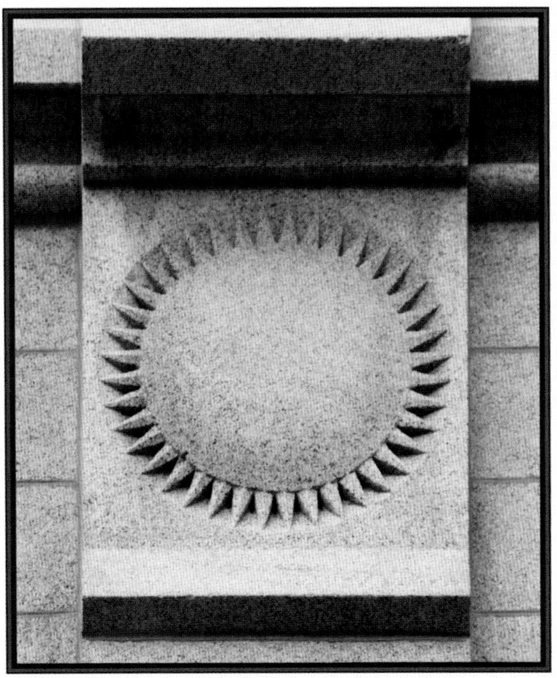

No other image represents The Church of Jesus Christ of Latter-day Saints in the minds of people both in and out of the Church as well as the Salt Lake Temple. Nor is there another temple in the Church that combines so many of the common exterior symbols used on LDS temples. Temples are a great gift from God that remind the Saints that He loves them, that He offers them His grace, and that the Atonement and exaltation are the greatest of all His gifts (see D&C 14:7).

The most obvious features of the Salt Lake Temple are the sets of three ascending towers on the east and the west fronts, which encourage God's children to remember the gift of exaltation and which inspire them to maintain the constant climb to perfection and godlike character that is taught in the endowment. The two sets of towers also represent two more great gifts from God: the presidencies of the Melchizedek and Aaronic priesthoods. The eastern towers, which represent the First Presidency, are six feet higher than the western towers and have five windows, one more than the towers on the western side. The western towers represent the Presiding Bishopric, or the presidency of the Aaronic Priesthood. Also, since twelve is often a number that represents priesthood, the twelve spires on each of the towers emphasize the fact that it is the priesthood of God that administers the ordinances of exaltation and points our way to heaven.

Both the gift of priesthood and the path to heaven, as well as the encouragement to have an eternal perspective, continue with the representation of heavenly bodies on all sides of the temple. The celestial bodies on the Salt Lake Temple are in the same order as they are on the Nauvoo Temple except that earth stones—circles encased in squares—have been added at the base of the temple. The original architectural drawings indicate that these stones were originally supposed to feature carved continents[48] rotating on their axes, making the temple the symbolical center of the earth for Latter-day Saints. Ascending upward from the earth stones, the temple displays moons, suns, and stars on its different levels, imitating again, as at Nauvoo, the visible universe.

According to scholar Richard Oman,[49] the forty five-pointed stars, found only on the three eastern towers, may refer also to God's gift of priesthood to guide us, in that they may represent the great and noble spirits of premortality whom God assigned to be rulers in His kingdom.

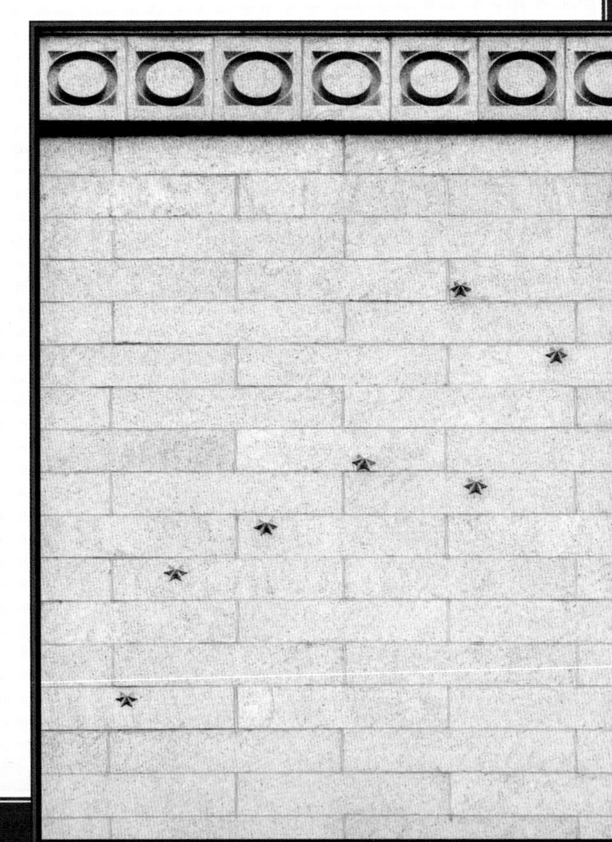

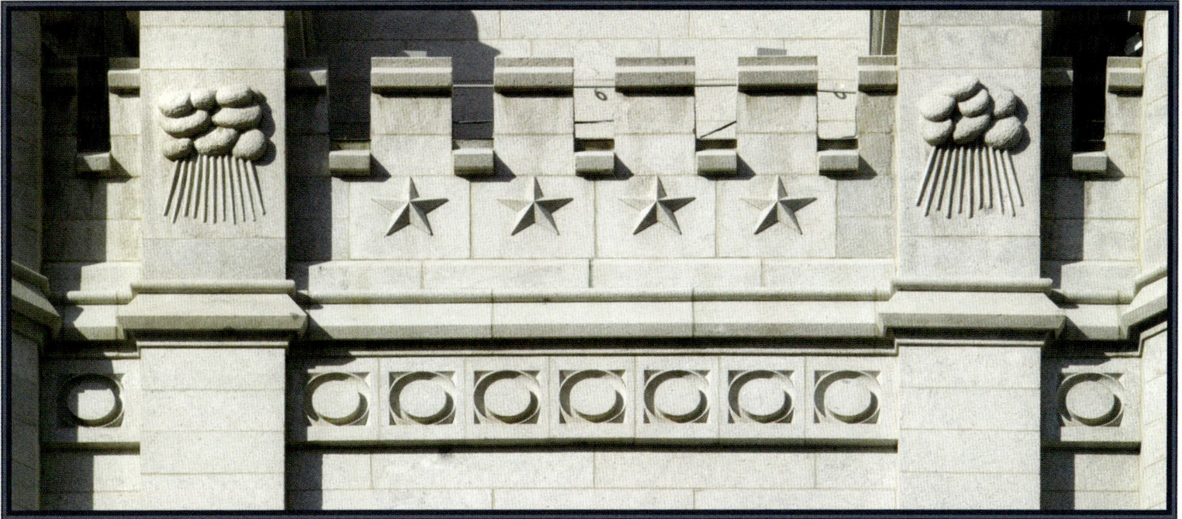

A related symbol unique to the east central towers are the two cloud stones to the right and left of the stars, representing the light from God given to the earth through the restoration of priesthood keys and gospel truth.

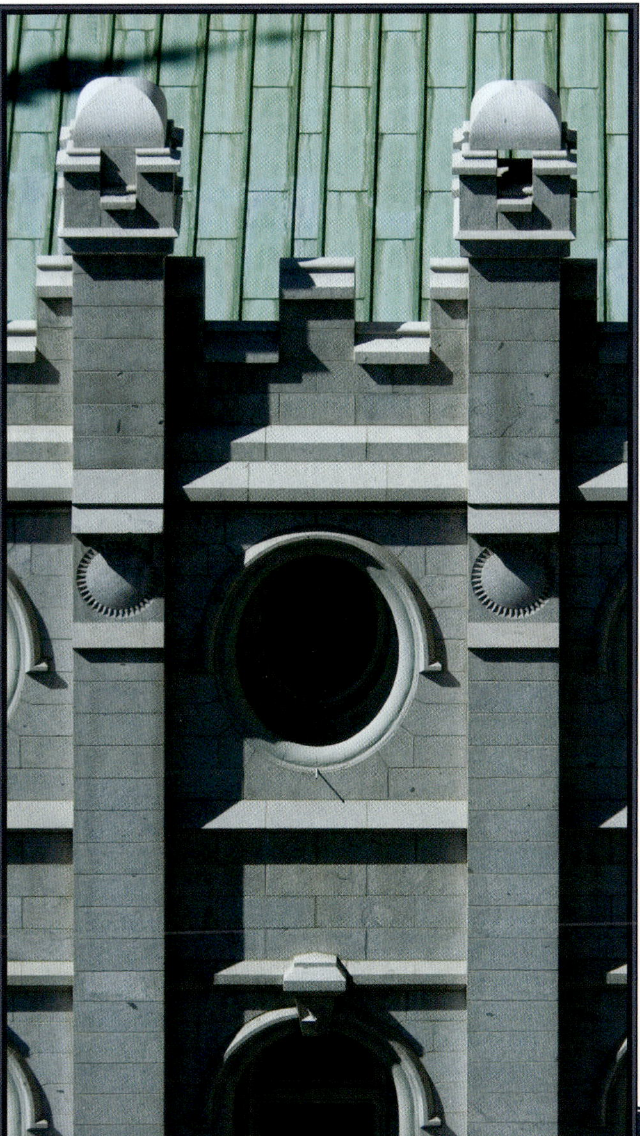

A similar feature found only on the central western tower, the Big Dipper (the constellation that points to the North star and allows travelers to take their bearings) also points to the gift of priesthood and its ordinances as the means by which men and women can find their way back to God.

The gift of God's protection is symbolically displayed in two ways in the Salt Lake Temple architecture. First, the niches surrounding the eastern doors originally, until 1911, housed the statues of Joseph and Hyrum Smith acting as cherubim to guard the temple from all evil. Second, the battlements that decorate the highest reaches of the temple portray the Salt Lake Temple as a mighty fortress against evil.

Finally, God offers His children fellowship and an ever-watchful vigilance. The Salt Lake Temple symbolizes these offers of God's love with fellowshipping hands and an all-seeing eye. He will guide us and watch over us and help us keep our covenants. And eventually, by His grace, He will exalt us in His kingdom, a true gift from a loving Father.

perfected in Him, through His grace, that we can receive a remission of our sins and be made holy. It is, in short, the summation of the eight exhortations that began with a plea to remember the mercies of God. He has made his case that we must not deny the good gifts that God offers us.

The term *endowment* means "gift," or something that is given or bestowed. It correctly describes what Heavenly Father does for His children in the temple ceremony. The term should remind us that in the temple God offers us a gift of knowledge and perspective. He offers us protection from evil. Most importantly, He offers us a preparation for the greatest of all of His gifts, eternal life (see D&C 14:7). Through its symbolic

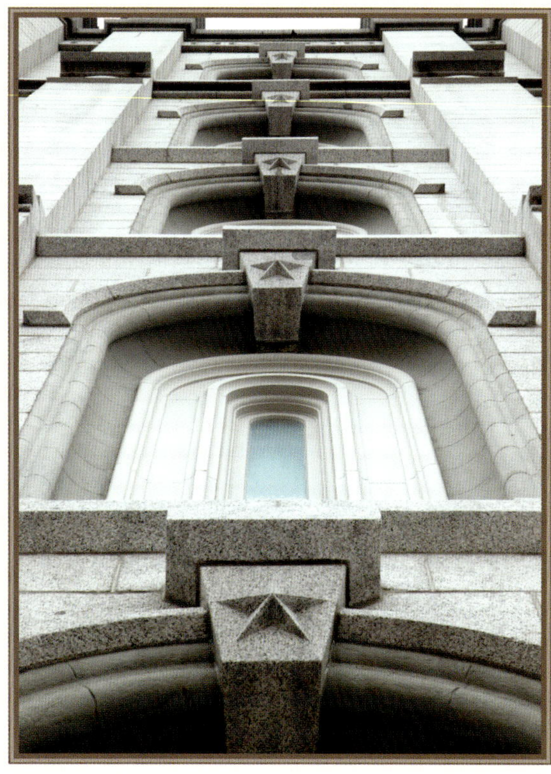

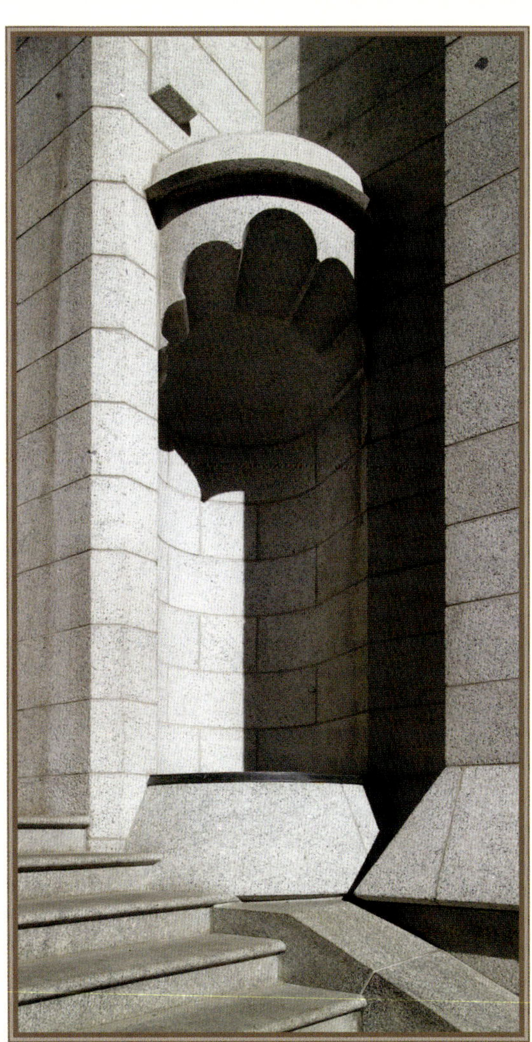

message, the temple instructs the Saints concerning the eternal journey to exaltation. As Elder James E. Talmage explained, temple patrons move from a garden room to a world room, then to a terrestrial room, and finally through a veil to the celestial room.[50] Latter-day Saints understand that this movement represents progression from the innocence of childhood to the natural-man condition of temptation and sin in the fallen world we live in, to the possibility of repentance and atonement symbolized by the terrestrial room, and finally to exaltation in the celestial glory as one enters into the presence of God. Furthermore, the endowment goes beyond the instruction and administers the covenants that make the Atonement effective on its highest levels. In short, it is the means by which God's children fully come unto Christ.

It would indeed be foolish to reject the amazing gift of the temple endowment, given its breadth and depth. Unfortunately, mortal men and women do not always do

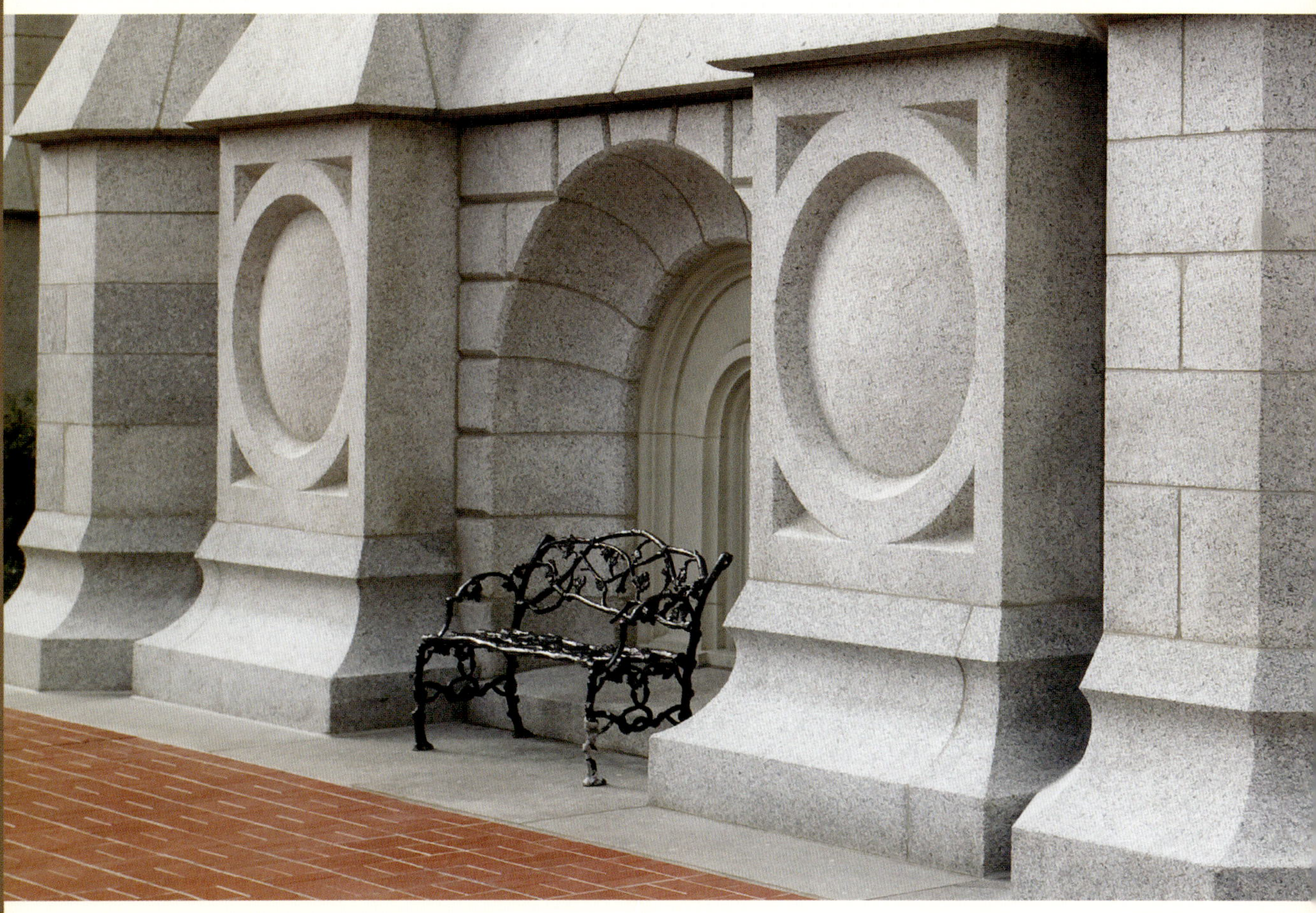

what is good for them, and not all good gifts are used properly. God offered Cain, for instance, a second chance at having his sacrifice accepted, but Cain rejected it (see Moses 5:22–23). God gave the people of Noah's day 120 years to repent, but they refused to listen (see Moses 8:17). He gave Pharaoh nine different warnings before the tenth plague took the firstborn of Egypt, but Pharaoh continually hardened his heart (see the JST footnotes for Exodus 7:3, 13; 10:1, 27; 11:10; 14:4, 8). As these selected examples show, many of God's children foolishly deny His gifts.

The endowment is another case in point. Not all who participate in the ceremony honor or utilize it. To make the promises of the endowment operational, we must keep the covenants entered into during that ceremony. The covenants commit us to keeping the conditions of eternal life. Honoring them signifies that we have used our agency to accept God's help, allowing God to work with us, to form us, and to mold us to be in His own image. Little by little He creates in us a new person, one who is born again. Not keeping our covenants means we are not using the gift. Therefore, accepting this gift called the endowment and using it wisely leads to full sanctification in the next life, while denying it leads to one level or another of damnation.

The endowment is God's best teaching tool because it sets up a template by which we can analyze mortality. In a world that is mostly a testing ground for eternity, the temple is a vision into eternity that reminds us who we are, where we came from, why we are here, and what God expects of us.

Notes

Journey to the Tree of Life

1 John A. Widtsoe, *A Rational Theology* (Salt Lake City: Deseret Book, 1965), 125–26. Quoted in *Ensign,* February 1995, 40.

2 "Endowment," *Encyclopedia of Mormonism* (New York: Macmillan, 1992), 2:455.

3 See Jack Tresidder, *Dictionary of Symbols* (San Francisco: Chronicle Books, 1997), 82.

4 See Revelation 22:2, also Tresidder, *Dictionary of Symbols,* 212.

5 Rudger Clawson, in Conference Report, April 1937, 74.

The "Good/Evil Contrast" Pattern

6 To clearly understand this portion of the vision, it is useful to remember the Book of Mormon definition for the term "Gentile nations." The Book of Mormon consistently defines Gentiles as anyone from a nation other than the political kingdom of Judah or Israel. A Jew, on the other hand, is anyone who is from the ancient kingdom of Judah or Israel or is a descendent of those who lived within that kingdom. These are political designations.

To clarify, a Gentile is anyone who lives in a nation other than the kingdoms of Israel and Judah and who is not descended primarily from those who lived in those same kingdoms. In this sense, Lehi and Nephi are Jews because they come from Jerusalem, and by extension so are all of the Nephites and Lamanites (because they are descendants of Jews). Even though these peoples are not primarily from the tribe of Judah, they are originally from the nation of Judah.

On the other hand, Christ tells the Nephites that the Book of Mormon will be brought forth by the Gentiles (see 1 Nephi 13:35; 3 Nephi 21:6), because most of the members of the last dispensation, Joseph Smith included, are citizens of modern Gentile countries and not descended from those who lived in the kingdom of Judah. They are covenant Israelites because they have made covenants that enable them to be adopted into the house of Israel, but they are political Gentiles because they live in Gentile nations.

Elder Bruce R. McConkie provides an informative historical summary of how these designations came to be:

> In the days of Abraham, the term [Gentile] was used to refer to those nations and peoples who had not descended from him, with the added assurance that all Gentiles who should receive the gospel should be adopted into the lineage of Abraham and be accounted his seed. (Abra. 2:9–11.) The Prophet taught that those so adopted became literally of the blood of Abraham. (*Teachings,* pp. 149–150.) In the days of ancient Israel, those not of the lineage of Jacob were considered to be Gentiles, although the Arabs and other races of Semitic origin who traced their lineage back to Abraham would not have been Gentiles in the strict Abrahamic use of the word.
>
> After the Kingdom of Israel was destroyed and the Ten Tribes were led away into Assyrian captivity, those of the Kingdom of Judah called themselves Jews and designated all others as Gentiles. It is this concept that would have been taught to Lehi, Mulek and the other Jews who came to the Western Hemisphere to found the great Nephite and Lamanite civilizations.

> It is not surprising, therefore, to find the Book of Mormon repeatedly speaking of Jew and Gentile as though this phrase marked a division between all men; to find the United States described as a Gentile Nation (1 Ne. 13; 3 Ne. 21); and to find the promise that the Book of Mormon would come forth "by way of the Gentile." (Title page of Book of Mormon; D. & C. 20:9.)
>
> Actually, of course, the house of Israel has been scattered among all nations, and Joseph Smith (through whom the Book of Mormon was revealed) was of the Tribe of Ephraim. At the same time the Prophet was of the Gentiles, meaning that he was a citizen of a Gentile Nation and also that he was not a Jew. (Bruce R. McConkie, *Mormon Doctrine* [Salt Lake City: Bookcraft, 1966], 311.)

Gathering to the Family of God

7 Joseph Fielding Smith, *Answers to Gospel Questions* (Salt Lake City: Deseret Book, 1960), 3:152–54.

8 Joseph Fielding Smith, *Doctrines of Salvation,* comp. Bruce R. McConkie (Salt Lake City: Bookcraft, 1955), 3:129.

9 *Teachings of the Prophet Joseph Smith* (Salt Lake City: Deseret Book, 1977), 307–8.

10 Russell M. Nelson, "The Gathering of Scattered Israel," *Ensign,* November 2006, 81.

11 George A. Smith, in *Journal of Discourses* (London, England: Latter-day Saints' Book Depot, 1854–86), 2:214.

12 The following brief summary of the Isaiah chapters in 1 Nephi is offered as an aid to comprehension and a testimony that the doctrine of the gathering preaches the power of the Atonement:

20:1–8 The wicked of the covenant people—those who have been baptized and who claim they follow God but do not stay, or depend, on Him—are called to repentance. God has spoken to them ancient things and new things in hopes that they will believe Him and not follow idols and false gods. Israel does not listen.

20:9–11 God promises that He will, for His own purposes, redeem Israel, after He has tried them in the furnace of affliction, after they have faced the consequences of their decisions to scatter themselves spiritually.

20:12–19 God calls Israel to listen to Him. He does, after all, have great power—enough, even, to create the earth. Surely the people must acknowledge that He has the power to save His people. They must trust Him. God has loved those who have taught and announced the Redemption. He will destroy Babylon, a symbol of wickedness. God has spoken and has called others to declare the way. God tells Israel that He wishes they would have listened, because if they had, He would have been able to bless them.

20:20–22 If Israel will repent, God will redeem them and bless them. But He will not help the wicked.

21:1–3 God tells Israel to pay attention, that He has called His servant (Christ) and given Him power.

21:4–5 The servant responds that He has surely labored in vain. Israel has not listened. The servant declares that in spite of His lack of success, at least He has done what God has required of Him. Therefore, God will give Him glory.

21:6–7 God responds to the servant with irony. He tells Him that He indeed will save Israel. But this work will eventually be considered a light thing, a small thing. In the end, He will not only save Israel, but He will also be the means of salvation for the Gentiles in all the earth.

21:8–13 God promises Israel a joyful gathering, one accomplished with singing and blessings.

21:14–21 Zion personified will say, "God has forgotten me." But God will show that He has not. A woman with a nursing baby will forget her own child before God will forget Zion. There will be so many people converting and coming to the covenants of Israel that even the desert places will be crowded. So many people will join Israel through covenant that Zion personified will say, "Where did all these children come from?"

21:22–26 God will use the Gentiles (Joseph Smith and others) to restore the gospel and to bring the blessings of the temple back to Israel. The captives (those without spiritual enlightenment) will be delivered. Israel—covenant-keeping Saints—will be blessed and led and protected.

Returning to the Tree of Life

13 Ezra Taft Benson, "The Book of Mormon and the Doctrine and Covenants," *Ensign,* May 1987, 85.

14 Though Lehi begins the chapter by addressing just Jacob (see 2 Nephi 2:2), by the end of the chapter he seems to be addressing more than just one of his sons (see 2 Nephi 2:28).

15 "These three divine events [Creation, Fall, Atonement]—the three pillars of eternity—are inseparably woven together into one grand tapestry known as the eternal plan of salvation" (Bruce R. McConkie, *A New Witness for the Articles of Faith* [Salt Lake City: Deseret Book, 1985], 81).

16 Moses 3–4 is Joseph Smith's inspired version of Genesis 2–3.

17 The words in Hebrew for "help meet," *ezer kinnegdo,* mean just what has been explained—a noun and an adjective that mean "help appropriate."

18 Bruce R. McConkie, "Christ and the Creation," in Robert L. Millett and Kent P. Jackson, *Studies in Scripture: The Pearl of Great Price* (Salt Lake City: Randall Book Co., 1985), 2:88.

19 *The Teachings of Spencer W. Kimball* (Salt Lake City: Bookcraft, 1995), 68.

20 Joseph Fielding Smith, Address to LDS Institute of Religion, Salt Lake City, January 14, 1961, copy in author's possession.

21 See "transgress" in *Webster's New Collegiate Dictionary* (Springfield, MA: G. & C. Merriam Company, 1975).

22 Spencer W. Kimball, "The Lord's Plan for Men and Women," *Ensign,* October 1975, 5.

23 *Sermons and Writings of Ezra Taft Benson* (Salt Lake City: The Church of Jesus Christ of Latter-day Saints, 2003), 217.

24 The First Presidency and Council of the Twelve Apostles, "The Family: A Proclamation to the World," *Ensign,* November 1995, 102.

Covenants and Ascension to God

25 Joseph Smith and B. H. Roberts, *History of the Church* (Salt Lake City: Deseret Book, 1909), 5:424.

26 Neal A. Maxwell, "The Inexhaustible Gospel," *Ensign,* April 1993, 68.

27 Marion G. Romney, "Temples—the Gates to Heaven," *Ensign,* March 1971, 16.

28 Bible Dictionary, "Abraham, Covenant of," 602.

29 *Teachings of the Prophet Joseph Smith* (Salt Lake City: Deseret Book, 1977), 150.

Rebirth

30 Hugh Nibley suggests that the "wrestling" is probably a ritual embrace: "One of the most puzzling episodes in the Bible has always been the story of Jacob's wrestling with the Lord. When one considers that the word conventionally translated as 'wrestled' (yeaveq) can just as well mean 'embrace,' and that it was in this ritual embrace that Jacob received a new name and the bestowal of priestly and kingly power at sunrise (Gen 32:24–30), the parallel to the Egyptian coronation embrace becomes at once apparent" (Hugh Nibley, *Message of the Joseph Smith Papyri: An Egyptian Endowment* [Salt Lake City: Deseret Book, 2005], 434).

31 Bill Lewis, personal interview by Val Brinkerhoff, August 11, 2006.

32 See Hugh Nibley, *Temple and Cosmos* (Salt Lake City: Deseret Book, 1992), 109.

33 Lorenzo Snow, "Blessings of the Gospel Only Obtained by Compliance to the Law," *Ensign,* October 1971, 18.

34 Dallin H. Oaks, "Taking Upon Us the Name of Christ," *Ensign,* May 1985, 82.

Eternal Perspectives

35 John A. Widtsoe, *A Rational Theology* (Salt Lake City: Deseret Book, 1965), 125–26; quoted in *Ensign,* February 1995, 40.

36 James E. Talmage, *The House of the Lord* (Salt Lake City: Deseret Book, 1969), 111.

37 Boyd K. Packer, in Conference Report, October 1986, 20; see also *Ensign,* November 1986, 17.

The Law of the Gospel and the Covenant

38 A good starting point for more information on Mount Sinai as a temple is Donald W. Parry, "Sinai as Sanctuary and Mountain of God," in *By Study and Also by Faith: Essays in Honor of Hugh W. Nibley,* J. Lundquist and S. Ricks, eds. (Salt Lake City and Provo, Utah: Deseret Book and FARMS, 1990), 482–500.

39 Some people object that the visit of the seventy-three elders to Mount Sinai could not have been a temple experience, preparatory to the Second Comforter, because Aaron did not hold the Melchizedek Priesthood. However, John Taylor tells us that he did:

> By what power did Aaron see God? May we not suppose it was by the power of the Melchizedec Priesthood? For without that no man can see the face of God and live. It, the Melchizedec, holds the keys of the mysteries of the kingdom, even the key of the knowledge of God. . . . Moses had these keys; but Aaron also saw God, as well as the seventy elders of Israel. . . .
>
> It would seem that Aaron and the seventy elders of Israel then had the Melchizedec Priesthood (John Taylor, "Items on Priesthood," Priesthood Meeting, Oct. 9, 1880, pamphlet, 1881, 5; quoted in Lee A. Palmer, *Aaronic Priesthood through the Centuries* [Salt Lake City: Deseret Book, 1964], 19).

40 Israel's reaction to hearing God's voice at the time of the Ten Commandments had foreshadowed this rejection: "And they said to Moses, Speak thou with us, and we will hear: but let not God speak with us, lest we die" (Exodus 20:19). This fear, coupled with disobedience, cost them the blessing of the law

of the gospel and the Melchizedek Priesthood temple ordinances. As Joseph Smith taught, "The Israelites prayed that God would speak to Moses and not to them; in consequence of which he cursed them with a carnal law" (*Teachings of the Prophet Joseph Smith* [Salt Lake City: Deseret Book, 1977], 322).

41 See John W. Welch, *The Sermon at the Temple and the Sermon on the Mount* (Salt Lake City: Deseret Book, 1990), 34–83.

42 Ezra Taft Benson, "What I Hope You Will Teach Your Children about the Temple," *Ensign,* August 1985, 8.

43 Keith Stepan, personal interview by Val Brinkerhoff, December 8, 2006.

Entering the Presence of God

44 The other fifty-seven verses give short instructions to Joseph Smith as the eventual translator, describe how faith will bring men and women into the presence of God, and describe the New Jerusalem.

45 Catherine Thomas, "The Brother of Jared at the Veil," in Donald Parry, ed., *Temples of the Ancient World* (Salt Lake City and Provo, Utah: Deseret Book and FARMS, 1977), 388–98.

46 For more on this issue, see the last two chapters of Bruce R. McConkie, *The Promised Messiah* (Salt Lake City: Deseret Book, 1995).

47 *Teachings of the Prophet Joseph Smith* (Salt Lake City: Deseret Book, 1977), 150.

The Gifts of God

48 See Richard G. Oman, "Exterior Symbolism of the Salt Lake Temple: Reflecting the Faith That Called the Place into Being," *BYU Studies,* 1996–97, 36:4:24.

49 For more information on the symbols of the Salt Lake Temple, see Oman, "Exterior Symbolism of the Salt Lake Temple," 36:4:6, and Matthew B. Brown and Paul Thomas Smith, *Symbols in Stone: Symbolism on the Early Temples of the Restoration* (American Fork, UT: Covenant Communications, 1997).

50 See James E. Talmage, *The House of the Lord* (Salt Lake City: Deseret Book, 1969), 156–60.

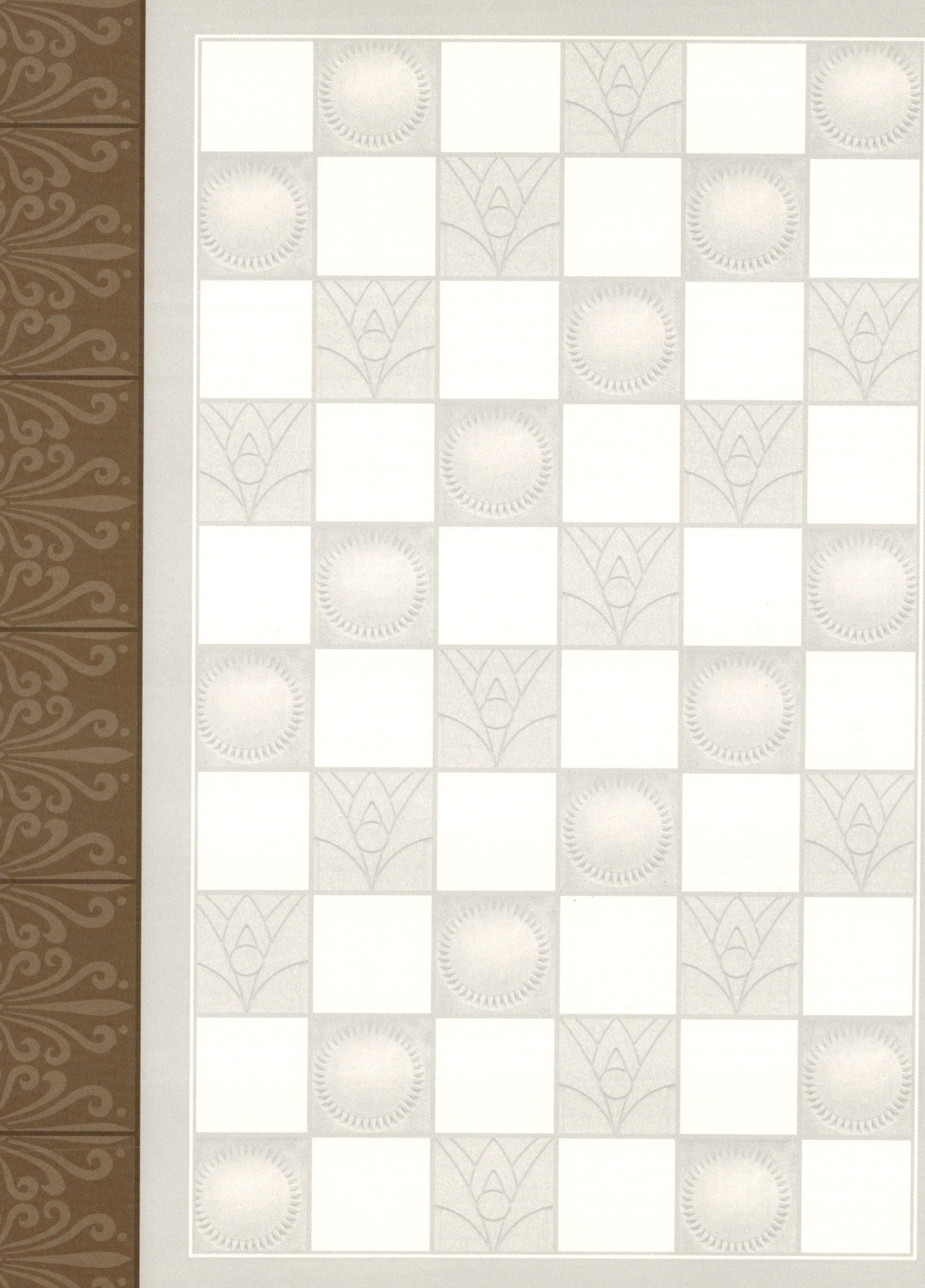

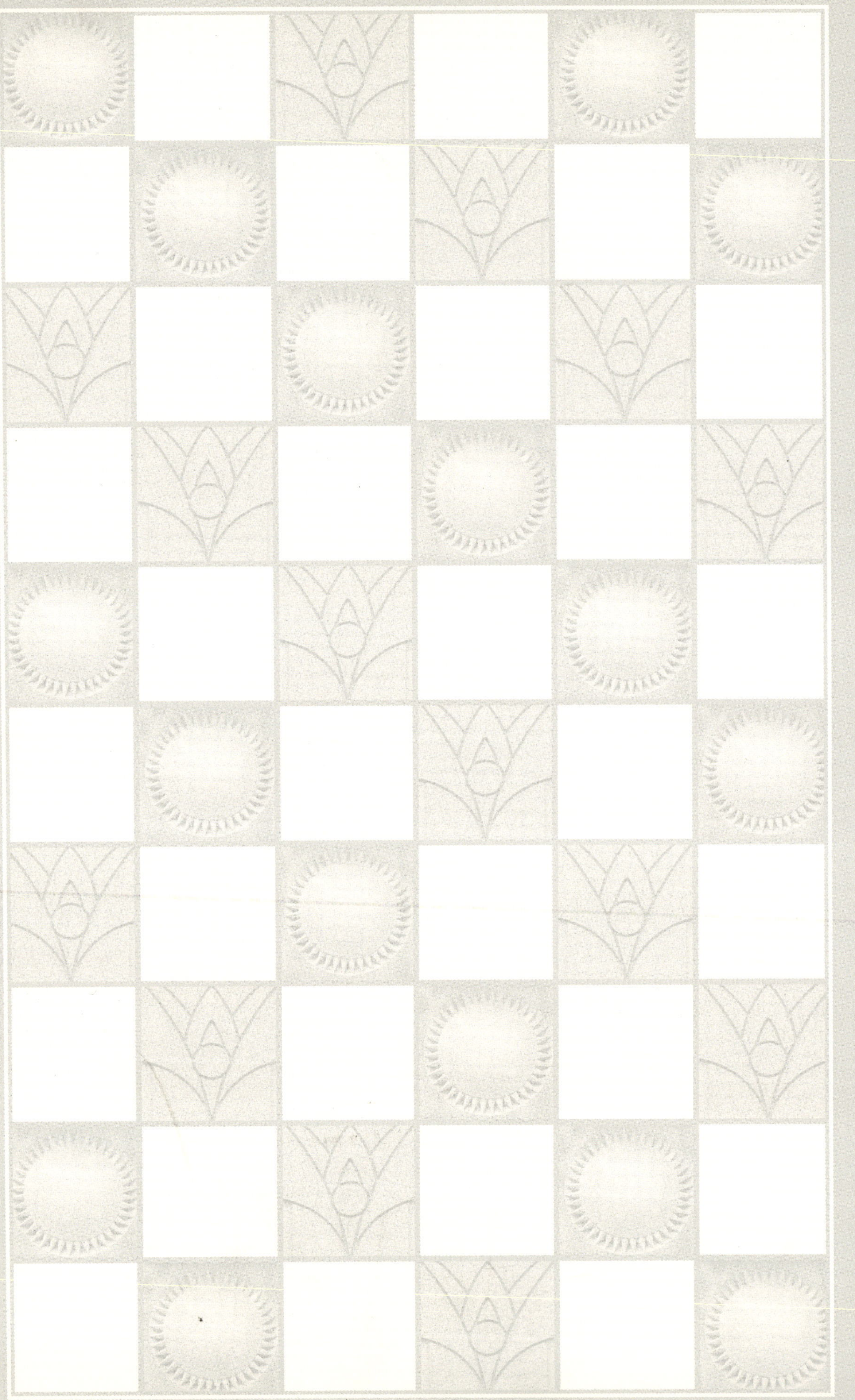